Literary Discussion in the Elementary School

Literary Discussion in the Elementary School

Joy F. Moss
The Harley School, Rochester, New York
University of Rochester, New York

National Council of Teachers of English
1111 W. Kenyon Road, Urbana, Illinois 61801-1096

Staff Editor: Tom Tiller

Interior Design: Doug Burnett

Cover Design: Jenny Jensen Greenleaf

NCTE Stock Number: 29633-3050

It is the policy of NCTE in its journals and other publications to provide a forum for the open discussion of ideas concerning the content and the teaching of English and the language arts. Publicity accorded to any particular point of view does not imply endorsement by the Executive Committee, the Board of Directors, or the membership at large, except in announcements of policy, where such endorsement is clearly specified.

Library of Congress Cataloging-in-Publication Data

Moss, Joy F., 1937–
    Literary discussion in the elementary school / Joy F. Moss.
        p. cm.
Includes bibliographical references (p.   ) and index.
    ISBN 0-8141-2963-3 (pbk.)
  1. Literature—Study and teaching (Elementary) 2. Group reading
3. Children—Books and reading.   I. Title.
    LB1575 .M677 2002
    372 . 64—dc21

                                                          2002005449

To Daniel, Rachel, Aaron, Yonah, Adam,
Julia, Joshua, Tamar, and Emily—
another generation of book lovers.

Contents

Preface

The study of literature *in its own right* is a valid and valuable experience in the elementary school. This is the central premise of *Literary Discussion in the Elementary School*. The purpose of this book is to suggest ways to develop rich and diverse literary experiences that provide students with opportunities to become immersed in the study of literature and to discover the pleasures of exploring this treasurehouse of language and ideas. At the heart of the exploration of literature is literary discussion. Literature serves as a springboard for talk in the social context of the classroom. In response to shared literary texts, children reflect on their experience with the text and talk about their thoughts and feelings, their associations and memories, their questions and concerns. As children share their personal responses to literary texts, they also consider the responses, understandings, and questions of others. They explore the multiple perspectives of group members and the layers of meaning uncovered as these diverse individuals respond to a shared text. As they collaborate to construct meanings together, children discover the multiple interpretations that a single text can generate. As they engage in literary analysis, children identify authors' craft as well as literary techniques that authors use to elicit reader response. Talk about literature opens up paths of intellectual inquiry that lead to explorations of important issues and insights about human values, motivations, behaviors, and interactions, about personal responsibility and consequences of one's deeds. Talk about literature leads to deeper understandings about a particular text, about literature in general, and about life.

The content of this book grew out of my personal experiences both as a student of literature and of literary/literacy learning and as a teacher of young children for thirty years. I have had the good fortune to work with and observe children as they experience literature, engage in literary study, and discover the joys of exploring literary texts in the social context of the classroom. Each chapter in this book includes excerpts from actual literary discussions that evolved in the context of cumulative read-aloud sessions in which children listened to and discussed shared texts. These excerpts illustrate the nature of literary talk before and after a story is presented as well as during the unfolding of the narrative.

The children quoted in this book were, unless otherwise stated, my students. However, I have chosen to use the third person throughout this text to refer to myself as the teacher whose voice is heard in the excerpts, along with references to the few other teachers quoted in the text. One reason for the use of the third person is to provide continuity in this text. Another reason for this choice is related to my dual role as an educator and a student of education. To promote my own growth and effectiveness as a teacher in the classroom, I make it a habit to step back from my own practice to reflect on "what happened." That is, I view the classroom experience with a critical lens as I move from a subjective to an objective stance or a "third-person" perspective. Viewing what happened in the classroom with this critical lens enables me to consider the experience in light of my instructional goals, the needs and progress of individual children, and relevant theory and research that has informed my practice. The art of teaching evolves out of an ongoing process of reflection and evaluation conducted before, during, and after one implements instructional plans in the classroom. After my own plans for a literary experience have been translated into practice, I step back from the experience for reflection and objective evaluation. With a critical lens, I assess the quality of each child's responses to the shared text and his/her involvement in and contribution to the collaborative process of constructing meaning and exploring multiple interpretations in the ongoing dialogue that is the core of the literature program. As a student of the teaching-learning relationship, I also assess my own role in this experience. This objective assessment provides the basis for planning subsequent group sessions as well as work with individual students. Thus, my practice is fluid and flexible in the context of this continuous reflection and learning.

The cumulative dialogue in the read-aloud sessions serves as the core of the literature program I have been developing for and with my students over the years. The nature of this program continues to evolve as I respond to the changing needs and interests of each new group of students and to utilize new publications in the world of children's literature. In the group sessions, the children are invited to enter into the story world together, to respond to each story as it unfolds, and to share their thoughts and feelings and understandings at the completion of the story. Following their subjective responses, the children engage in an objective analysis of the story and a comparative analysis of the diverse stories introduced in the course of a carefully planned sequence of read-aloud sessions. In this comparative-analysis approach to literary study, the children are invited to consider each new text in light of all previous texts introduced in these literature sessions and to use intertextual links to generate meaning. The literature program featured in this book is grounded in theories of literary and literacy learning and reader response and is intended to introduce children to the rich and expanding world of literature.

The content of this book has also grown out of my work as a teacher educator. For thirty years, I have taught classroom teachers as well as preservice teachers. As a teacher educator, I have explored with my students the field of children's literature, theories of literary/literacy learning, and ways to translate this knowledge into practice. This blend of experiences—teaching and learning from children and teachers—enabled me to write this book about literary discussion in the classroom.

Acknowledgments

I would like to express my deep appreciation to Sid S. Glassner, the former publisher and editor of the journal *Teaching and Learning Literature with Children and Young Adults*. He suggested that I write a series of articles about literary discussion for his journal; the introductory article for this series was published in the September/October 1998 issue of the journal. Unfortunately, that was the last issue of the journal and thus the end of the series. However, like the phoenix, the idea for a book about literary discussion emerged out of this unfinished project. So, I want to thank Sid Glassner for his support and encouragement and for providing the first step toward the publication of *Literary Discussion in the Elementary School*.

I would also like to thank Peter Feely and Tom Tiller at NCTE for their thoughtful involvement in the process, and the reviewers for their useful feedback that helped me to rethink and revise the early drafts of this manuscript.

Acknowledgment is due to all those who have journeyed with me into the world of literature over the years: my children and grandchildren; my students, young and old; and my colleagues. From all of them I have learned a great deal about literary experience and response, and their questions have challenged me to grow as a teacher and as a student of literature and learning.

Finally, I want to express my gratitude for the loving support of my family: my husband, Arthur; our children and their spouses—Kathy and Jeff, Debbie and Keith, Abby and David; and our grandchildren, Daniel, Rachel, Aaron, Yonah, Adam, Julia, Joshua, Tamar, and Emily.

1 Literary Discussion and the Quest for Meaning

The Boy Who Held Back the Sea (Hort, 1987) was read aloud to a group of fourth graders who had been invited to think about how authors create stories. The opening words of this unusual retelling of the famous legend of the Dutch boy and the dike[1] are: "Pieter had just been sent to his room and now there was a knock." These words prompted one student to ask, "But *why* was he sent to his room? Is something missing here?" The teacher responded by requesting help from the group.

> *Student #2:* "I think Pieter was probably bad. . . . That's why he was sent to his room."
>
> *Student #3:* "But the author just wants you to figure it out for yourself. . . . Like he doesn't give you *all* the details."
>
> *Student #4:* "I think he [the author] wants you to use your *own* experience to fill in the missing parts. . . . He gets you *into* the story . . . with a question!"
>
> *Student #5:* "And he can *choose* what to leave out!"
>
> *Student #1:* "Oh, I get it! But *what* did he do wrong that got him sent to his room?"[2]

At this point, the teacher commented, "That's a good question to think about as we listen to the rest of the story. The author may not give us a specific answer, but there are probably some clues to help us figure it out."

These fourth graders and their teacher were beginning a journey together. As they shared the pleasure of experiencing a good story together, they also shared in the process of searching for clues and constructing meaning as the story unfolded. The students had learned that reading is an *ongoing* process of meaning construction and that occasional interruptions *as a story unfolds* can be very useful for building understanding while listening to a text for the first time. The teacher's responsibility is two-fold: to create a safe environment in which students feel free to take risks and articulate questions or ideas prompted by the text, and, at the same time, to ensure that these occasional interruptions do not detract from the literary experience as a whole. Thus, the teacher's challenge is to maintain a delicate balance between giving children opportunities to share their thinking as active participants in the ongoing process of building understanding and enabling them to become fully engaged in the world of the story. The discussion of *The Boy Who Held Back the Sea* began with the children's thoughts about the title and picture on the front cover and continued with their response to the opening line and their comments at significant points *during* the unfolding of the story and *after* its conclusion. Excerpts from this ongoing literary discussion reveal the nature of the children's involvement in the story itself as well as the nature of their quest for understanding and their study of the author's craft:

> "I know what he [the author] did. . . . He took an old story that everybody knows and made a 'story-in-a-story'! It's just like that one we read last week [*The Wreck of the Zephyr*, Van Allsburg, 1983]."

> "When the boy ran to tell the people about the leak, I just *knew* they weren't going to believe him because he was always telling lies and trying to get attention. . . ."
> "It's just like the boy who cried wolf. . . ."
> "I know that story! It's a *fable*. . . . That's the kind that has the lesson at the end."
> "Maybe *that's* why Pieter's grandma told him the story about that other boy . . . to teach him a lesson . . . like a fable."
> "That's right! And that's the *clue*. . . . I think Pieter was sent to his room because he told lies . . . like the boy in the story!"
> "And so she [the grandmother] wanted to teach him a lesson: that if you lie, people won't ever believe you!"
> "But there's something else. . . . The grandma, I mean the *author*, added stuff to the old story. . . . The boy *changed* . . . from bad to good. . . . Remember at the end, he went to read to the blind man?"
> "I was so glad he did that . . . like he was probably thinking he didn't really *want* to be a bad kid."
> "So maybe that's the *other* part of her lesson . . . that *he* [Pieter] could change, too! And at the very end of the story, he *did*!"
> "That author makes you think and think. He leaves out stuff and you have to figure it out. . . . Like remember that book about the mysterious stone we read in second grade . . . and we all kept trying to figure out what the stone was. . . ."
> "I remember. . . . That was *The Wretched Stone* [Van Allsburg, 1991]. That's the kind of book I like. . . . You read it and it just keeps bugging you, and you can't stop thinking about it, and what it means. . . ."
> "Me too. I like it when the author keeps giving you clues in the story . . . about the characters and why they do things and what's going to happen. . . . Like when they didn't believe Jan. . . . You could just *predict* that . . . because of the clues he [the author] gave."

These children were clearly excited about this story experience and the challenges it offered them as engaged readers. They entered into the story together and then collaborated in the meaning-making process, building on the ideas of others to extend understandings and develop insights. The children talked about story characters and made inferences about the motives and internal responses of these characters; they used intertextual links with prior texts to generate meanings; they explored the craft of authors and reflected on their own experiences as readers.

The rich literary discussion that evolved in response to this brief picture book did not just *happen*. The teacher set the stage for this literary discussion through careful planning and preparation informed by research and theory in literary and literacy learning. The excerpts from this discussion are intended to serve as an introduction to the central focus of this book: exploring the nature of literary discussions in elementary school classrooms and the importance of these discussions in the lives of children.

Rethinking the Nature of Literary Discussion

In recent years, the nature of literary discussion in elementary school classrooms has received considerable attention among educators interested in literary and literacy learning. One of the editors of *Lively Discussions! Fostering Engaged Reading* (1996) referred to conventional forms of post-reading discussions as "recitation" rather than discussion—"there is no collaborative attempt to construct meaning: the answers are already known" (Almasi, p. 5). These traditional interactions are generally teacher-dominated and are characterized by literal questions that elicit right or wrong answers. Studies of classroom discussion have revealed that literature has generally been taught in an informational manner with assessment as the primary goal (Applebee, 1989).

A view of literary discussion that challenges this traditional format emphasizes the value of readers' personal responses to literary texts and of opportunities to talk about these responses. In this view of literary discussion, personal responses to literary texts serve as a starting point for studying literature in group settings. The transaction between a reader and a literary text is a unique, personal, and emotional experience in which the reader actively builds understanding and generates personal meanings (Rosenblatt, 1978). Readers are invited to share these personal experiences; to consider the responses, understandings, interpretations, and questions of others; and to construct new meanings together in the social context of the classroom. Students can build upon this group experience to expand, enrich, and rethink their initial transactions with literary texts as individual readers.

This view of literary discussion is presented in a number of texts in which the authors offer their own definitions of the nature of literary discussion. For example, Gambrell and Almasi define literary discussion as a "forum for collaboratively constructing meaning and for sharing responses" (1996, p. 2). Lea M. McGee (1996) uses the term "response-centered talk" to describe literary discussions whose "purpose is the discovery or construction of new understandings about literature" (p. 195). Stanley Fish (1980) uses the term "interpretive community" to describe a group of readers "who both share their idiosyncratic interpretations and negotiate a group-constructed view of a story or poem" (quoted in McGee, 1995, p. 108). Deborah Wells describes successful literature discussion groups in which the book and the readers' responses are the central focus. In these "grand conversations" children engage in genuine dialogue to explore important ideas and issues (Wells, 1995, pp. 132–139).

The author of this book (see Moss, 1995, 1996, 2000) uses the phrase "shared reading experiences" to describe literary discussions that are woven into read-aloud sessions. These discussions begin with comments, questions, and predictions triggered by the title and cover and continue during the unfolding of the story and after its conclusion. That is, the children are invited to enter into the story world together and to build understanding step-by-step, cover-to-cover, in an ongoing shared reading experience. When the teacher reads aloud, the students are not passive listeners. They are actively involved in this ongoing process of meaning making *as the text unfolds*. Don Holdaway (1979) introduced the term "shared reading" to describe a component of beginning reading instruction in which predictable books are enlarged as "Big Books" to allow a group of children to listen to a story and see the print as the teacher reads aloud to them. The children are invited to read along with the teacher, and, after repeated readings, they are able to read the book on their own. In contrast to Holdaway's "shared reading" that serves as a context for early literacy learning, the "shared reading experiences" featured in this book serve as a context for literary learning through literary discussions in which children collaborate to construct meaning in response to shared texts.

Judith Langer views reading as a process involving *envisionment building*:

> I use the term *envisionment* to refer to the understanding a reader
> has about a text—what the reader understands at a particular

> point in time, the questions she has, as well as hunches about
> how the piece will unfold. Envisionments develop as the reading
> develops. . . . What readers come away with at the end of the
> reading, I call the final envisionment. This includes what they
> understand, what they don't, and the questions they still have.
> The final envisionment is also subject to change with time, as the
> result of conversations with others, the reading of other works,
> or pondering and reflection. (Langer, 1990, p. 812)

As the story is read aloud, students develop their own envisionments;
as they gain new information from the unfolding text, they examine,
revise, and/or expand these envisionments. At relevant points during
the oral presentation of the story, students are invited to articulate questions and predictions that will contribute to envisionment building. At
the conclusion of the story, students share their personal responses and
final envisionments and consider other students' perspectives and interpretations that accord with or differ from their own. In this "interpretive community," students talk with each other and negotiate a
group-constructed view of the story. As a result of this collaborative
process, children have opportunities to enhance their own understandings of a text and to extend their "final envisionments."

Why Are These Literary Discussions Important?

As a solitary experience, reading can be enjoyable and meaningful.
However, most readers know that sharing books and authors with
friends or in a group can enrich and extend the reading experience. In
her book, *In the Middle: Writing, Reading, and Learning with Adolescents*
(1987), Nancie Atwell describes a moment of insight as she observed
two adults sitting for hours at her dining room table "gossiping" about
a favorite author. "It [opened] my eyes to the wonders of our dining
room table. It is a literate environment. Around it, people talk in all the
ways literate people discourse" (p. 19). This discovery led her to rethink
her reading curriculum: "Somehow, I had to get that table into my classroom and invite my eighth graders to pull up their chairs" (p. 20). Atwell
created an environment in which she and her students talked naturally
and spontaneously about reading and writing, "entering into literature
together" (p. 20).

In all parts of the United States, adults gather together in living
rooms or around dining room tables to discuss shared book experiences
in formal or informal book clubs formed in response to the need to talk
about books with other literate people. On playgrounds and in school
cafeterias, children talk about books and authors and make personal

connections with others who share their reading interests. In the context of these diverse book-talk communities, readers enjoy opportunities to share literary experiences with others. Members of these communities, young and old, are often motivated to read more widely and deeply and to extend their appreciation and understanding of literary texts they had enjoyed as solitary readers.

Teachers who build on this natural inclination to share reading experiences in a social context give their students opportunities to talk to each other about books and to share their personal responses, interpretations, and opinions with others in the social context of the classroom. These shared thoughts often trigger further ideas from other participants. As they listen to each other, students discover diverse personal responses to a shared text and multiple perspectives and interpretations. In the process, they learn from others and about others as unique individuals. Students learn to see the world through the eyes of those whose experiences, knowledge, and perspectives differ from their own, and they discover connections with those whose viewpoints, ideas, and experiences are similar to their own.

These literary discussions—whether in response to stories read aloud in a group setting or to texts read independently and then shared—are an integral part of the reading experience in the classroom. The teacher's responsibility is to introduce students to a rich world of language, ideas, and human experiences in the form of poetry, fable, myth, legend, folk and fairy tale, modern fantasy, contemporary and historical realism, biography and autobiography, and informational books. The teacher sets the stage for enjoyable literary experiences that enhance the quality of the students' response to and appreciation of literature; that challenge them to stretch their minds and imaginations and open their hearts; and that provide the linguistic and literary knowledge needed to generate deeper meaning. Literary selections that invite readers to engage with the text and to search for understanding offer the kinds of reading experiences that readers want to share with others. The fourth graders whose voices were recorded in the opening segment of this chapter were introduced to a story selected by their teacher. Their responses during the literary discussion suggested that they were fully engaged in this literary experience and were motivated to search for understanding and to collaborate with their peers in order to respond to the intellectual challenge inherent in this unusual retelling of an old story. Although the individual students in this group differed in terms of their competence and confidence as independent readers and writers, they *all* contributed thoughtful and relevant comments to the literary discussions in this shared reading experience.

Literary discussion in the classroom is also important as a context in which literary and literacy learning are supported. Lev Vygotsky's early studies of language acquisition and cognitive development revealed that language learning begins in social interaction and that dialogue facilitates literacy learning (Vygotsky, 1962/1986). Through genuine dialogue, teachers and students collaborate as they respond to literature, explore possibilities, and construct meanings together. These literary conversations offer students opportunities to discover new ways to think about literary texts, to enrich their own responses as readers, and to extend their language competence. The invitation to "think out loud" in the context of these literary conversations provides students with the opportunity to practice the strategies that readers use to build understanding in response to literary texts. Leslie Oster defines the think-aloud as "a technique in which students verbalize their thoughts as they read and thus bring into the open the strategies they are using to understand a text [Baumann, Jones, & Seifert-Kessell, 1993; Davey, 1983; and Wade, 1990]" (2001, p. 64).

Reading Comprehension Strategies

The construction of meaning in response to literary texts is learned, and the teacher plays a significant role in promoting and supporting this learning. In the context of literary discussions of shared-text experiences, the teacher demonstrates *meaning-making strategies* used by proficient readers, such as making connections to their own prior knowledge and experience, asking questions, making predictions, drawing inferences, filling in gaps in the narrative, identifying author's craft and literary devices, synthesizing ideas, exploring multiple layers of meaning, and monitoring understanding. In addition, the teacher facilitates meaning making by introducing the *literary language* used in literate discourse. Thus, for example, as students struggle to articulate their thoughts about character development in a particular story or about the technique used by the author to develop that character, the teacher introduces the literary language used to talk about literary elements and author's craft.

The Quest for Meaning: Analyzing Literary Discussion

A review of the excerpts from the fourth graders' literary discussion recorded above reveals the literary language and reading strategies that these students had learned to use in order to analyze and talk about literature and to generate meaning in response to literary texts. For example, when one student asked a question about the opening sentence, other students made connections to their personal experiences to make sense of this line. One student used her growing knowledge of literary terms to identify the author's craft. That is, she noted that the author had used the "story-within-a-story" device to create *The Boy Who Held Back the Sea.* When another student shared a prediction he had made about the way the people in the story would respond to the boy who found the leak in the dike, others made connections to their prior knowledge of a particular fable and the nature of this literary genre. This connection prompted a return to an earlier point in the story to make inferences about a character's motivation and to fill in gaps left by the author. These children had apparently learned that reading literature is not a linear journey and that the process of building understanding involves detours or returning to previous segments of the text to rethink initial questions, predictions, or interpretations as new information or connections lead them to new envisionments. They were learning to monitor their understanding, to reread, and to revise their thinking in response to gaps or deficiencies in their comprehension of the unfolding text. These students were beginning to discover that their literary histories coexisted with current reading experiences and that prior texts could be used to build understandings of current texts. The student who observed the change in the character in the embedded story revealed an awareness of the nature of a "dynamic character" and identified the relevant clues in the text to support his statement. This comment prompted another student to expand the group's earlier interpretation of the grandmother's motives for telling the story. As these students engaged in the process of building understandings and constructing meanings together, they also reflected on their own experiences as readers. Their comments suggested an appreciation of author's craft and an awareness of the choices authors make as they create stories and the techniques they use to elicit reader response. These students also revealed their awareness that reading is a fluid process in which the reader is actively involved in creating meaning before, during, and after his or her interaction with the text. The teacher who listens carefully to the voices of children during literary discussions learns a great deal about how they think, how they respond to literary texts, what meaning-making strategies they use, what they know about language and literature, and what they need to know to grow as thoughtful readers and writers.

Children's Books Cited

Dodge, Mary Mapes. (1865). *Hans Brinker, or the Silver Skates: A Story of Life in Holland.* New York: Scribner's.

Hort, Lenny, reteller. (1987). *The Boy Who Held Back the Sea.* Illustrated by Thomas Locker. New York: Dial.

Van Allsburg, Chris. (1983). *The Wreck of the Zephyr.* Boston, MA: Houghton Mifflin.

Van Allsburg, Chris. (1991). *The Wretched Stone.* Boston, MA: Houghton Mifflin.

2 Theory into Practice

Reader-Response Theory

The view of literary discussion presented in this book has been informed by theories of literary and literacy learning and reader response that have evolved since Louise Rosenblatt introduced her transactional theory of reading in 1938. Her early work served as trailblazer and guide for researchers and educators who have explored various aspects of readers' responses to literature. According to Rosenblatt, "reading is a transaction, a two-way process, involving a reader and a text at a particular time under particular circumstances" (1982, p. 268). The nature of this transaction is determined by the reader's stance or "mental set." Rosenblatt uses the term *efferent* to refer to the stance of the reader who "focuses on accumulating what is to be carried away at the end of the reading" (p. 269). She uses the term *aesthetic* to refer to the stance of the reader whose attention shifts inward, centering "on what is to be created *during* an *aesthetic* stance" (p. 269). The aesthetic reader enters into a story and "lives through" it as a personal and emotional experience. Readers who step into the world of the literary text create their own stories by bringing to the narrative their personal memories, feelings, beliefs, experiences, literary histories, and expectations. The term *critical/analytic* has been used to refer to a third stance defined as "a focus on a major dilemma or problem facing a character, a consideration of reasons for different courses of action, and appeals to the text for evidence and for interpretive context" (Chinn, Anderson, & Waggoner, 2001, pp. 381–382).

Excerpts from a discussion by first graders who responded to *The Foundling Fox* by Irina Korschunow (1984) illustrate the way participants shift between the aesthetic stance, the critical/analytic stance, and the efferent stance in the course of a shared reading experience. *The Foundling Fox* is the story of an orphan fox whose mother has been killed by a hunter and who is rescued by a vixen with three kits of her own. The vixen risks her life to save the foundling from a hound dog and a badger and to carry him on the long journey home to her den and her three kits. As the story unfolded during the read-aloud session, the children entered into the world of this courageous and tenderhearted vixen, experienced the tensions of her encounters with danger, and sighed with relief when she was home at last. In the course of the discussion, the children reflected on their emotional response to this "lived-through" experience and shifted to a critical/analytic stance to focus on the vixen's dilemma, the motivation behind her choices and actions, and the textual evidence to support their comments. Several children shifted briefly to an efferent stance as they shared their discoveries of new information about animal behaviors. In their initial responses to the story, most of the children focused on the vixen; only one child focused on the foundling fox:

> "That vixen was smart the way she got away from the dog . . . the hunting dog."
>
> "And she was really brave. That part when that badger was fighting with her was scary."
>
> "But she had love to make her strong. That's what it said [in the story]. That's why she could fight that big animal." [In response to this textual reference, the teacher reread the relevant segment in the story.]
>
> "Animals do that . . . to protect their children."
>
> "And she was so small. . . . I was afraid she'd get killed. I was glad she got home safe!"
>
> "She could have run away and left him but she didn't. She decided to keep going!"
>
> "She's like a hero!"
>
> "I was really worried about the little fox . . . that the vixen might drop him because she was so tired. But she really loved him, and she adopted him, and she taught the other kits to love him, too."
>
> "How did she do that?"
>
> "Remember? It said she licked all of them so they all had her smell on them. I didn't know that's why they lick their babies. Anyway, then that mean neighbor said, 'Why do you need an extra kit?' but the little fox wasn't *extra*; now he was her *own* child, and she said she loved them all the same."

For this boy, the little fox was the central character. As an adopted child himself, he explained the meaning of adoption to his classmates who listened with rapt attention as he shared his own sense of pride in having been chosen by his parents. He had created his own story by bringing to this text his personal experiences and feelings. Louise Rosenblatt calls for literature instruction that emphasizes aesthetic reading: "Precisely because every aesthetic reading of a text is a unique creation, woven out of the inner life and thought of the reader, the literary work of art can be a rich source of insight and truth" (1982, pp. 276–277).

Judith Langer also distinguishes between reading literature and reading to gain information (1994):

> A literary orientation . . . can be characterized as *exploring a horizon of possibilities*. It explores emotions, relationships, motives, and

reactions calling on all we know about what it means to be human. . . . A literary orientation is one of exploring horizons—where uncertainty is a normal part of response, and newfound understandings provoke still other possibilities. When the purpose of reading is primarily to share or gain information (as when students read science or social studies texts), the reader's orientation can be characterized as 'maintaining a point of reference.'" (pp. 204–205)

Teachers whose view of literary discussion is grounded in reader-response theory encourage their students to engage in aesthetic reading, to "live through" each story as a unique, personal, and emotional experience. Students are invited to reflect on their individual reading experiences and to articulate their responses, understandings, and interpretations in literary conversations with teachers and peers. As students respond to literature, explore possibilities, and construct meanings together, they learn to take different stances as readers, and they discover new ways to think about literary texts and to enrich their own responses as readers. According to Langer,

> participants in a community of literate thinkers . . . interiorize their various readings in a quest for personal meaning, examine the text and life in varying degrees from a critical perspective, and treat others' comments as having the potential to enrich (as well as challenge) their own understandings. They also know that they have the right to disagree, and that they are likely to modify if not change their ideas with time. (1995, p. 4)

Several of the children involved in the discussion of *The Foundling Fox* revealed that they had discovered new ways to think about this story as they considered the perspective of their classmate who had focused on the little fox as an adopted child:

> "Maybe the author *wanted* you to think about the little fox more . . . because of the title!"
>
> "At first I felt sorry for the little fox because he was all alone. . . . See [she points to the text and asks the teacher to reread the opening lines] that's how the story starts out, but the *action* was about the vixen . . . so then I got worried about her! But the little fox must have been so happy to have a mother!"
>
> "I didn't get that part about the neighbor at the end."
>
> "I didn't either. Could we read that again?"

Listening to this last segment of the story a second time in response to their classmate's comments about adoption enabled the children to grasp the implied meaning of this encounter between the vixen and her neighbor and to make the connection to adoption in human terms:

"The first part of the story was more about real animals, but I think that last part was like a conversation that humans would have."

"I think the neighbor was jealous, because the vixen had such cute babies."

"I have a friend who's adopted and his mom and dad love him all the same as the other kids . . . just like in the story."

"So it *is* about adoption. That last part really proves it."

"But I think it's also about a heroine, too. A lot of stories are about boys who do brave things, but this time it's a girl, and that's why *I* liked it so much."

This comment was offered by a girl who was willing to grant that adoption was an important theme in this story, but she held onto her own perspective about the vixen as the heroine. Most of the girls in the group commented on the heroic role of the vixen, and several returned to the text to point to the scenes in which she proved her courage, cunning, and determination:

"The vixen was so *small*, so she had to be *really* brave to fight the badger!"

"And love made her stronger! Remember that part in the story?" [She used the picture of the vixen and badger to locate the scene she wanted the teacher to read again: 'He was strong, and he was fast. But the vixen was also strong and because she was fighting for her foundling fox, she was even stronger. She fought with her head and with her heart'(p. 28).]

"And she was so smart! Remember that part when she figured out how to escape from the hunting dog?" [This child also used a picture to locate the scene in which the vixen jumped into a stream and swam to the other side so the dog could not find her scent.]

In a summary of the work of Louise Rosenblatt, Edmund Farrell includes this important point: "Though students should be allowed to express freely their reactions to a selection in both writing and class discussions, a process that will help them clarify their responses, the text must remain a constraint against total relativism or subjectivity" (Farrell & Squire, 1990, p. x). The children who discussed *The Foundling Fox* had been encouraged by their teacher in earlier discussions to return to the text to support their interpretations and opinions. As the children reflected on their own responses to this story and explored multiple layers of meaning inherent in this story, they returned to the text to locate specific scenes that would support their arguments or interpretations.

According to Rosenblatt, "the reader can begin to achieve a sound approach to literature only when he reflects upon his response to it,

when he attempts to understand what in the work and in himself produced that reaction, and when he thoughtfully goes on to modify, reject, or accept it" (1938/1976, p. 76). In addition to reflecting on the text
and what they brought to it from their personal histories, beliefs, experiences, and feelings, these first graders considered the contributions
of other readers in order to extend their understandings and construct
new meanings. As aesthetic readers, these young students participated
in "the human experience" of literature:

> Certainly to the great majority of readers, the human experience
> that literature presents is primary. . . . The reader seeks to partici-
> pate in another's vision—to reap knowledge of the world, to
> fathom the resources of the human spirit, to gain insights that
> will make his own life more comprehensible. (Rosenblatt, 1938/
> 1976, p. 7)

The responses of young children to literary experiences reveal a
great deal about their personal beliefs, experiences, feelings, and understandings and can often provide adults with windows into the inner worlds of children. In her book, *Wally's Stories: Conversations in the
Kindergarten* (1981), Vivian Paley describes her own "search for the
child's point of view" (p. 213) through an ongoing record of her students' responses to picture books and fairy tales, as well as their original stories, which they dictated to the teacher. These stories were read,
reread, and acted out again and again in the classroom. For example,
the children's response to *Tico and the Golden Wings* (Lionni, 1964)
seemed to be shaped by their belief in justice and fairness. This is the
story of Tico, a wingless bird, who is cared for by his friends. However,
when a wishingbird grants his wish for golden wings, his friends are
angry. They said, "'You think you are better than we are, don't you, with
those golden wings. You wanted to be *different*.' And off they flew without saying another word" (unpaged). When Tico gives away his golden
feathers to those in need, he discovers that black feathers replace each
of the golden ones until his wings are black. Only then do his friends
return to him because "'Now you are just like us.'" The story ends with
Tico's inner thoughts: "'Now my wings are black . . . and yet I am not
like my friends. We are *all* different. Each for his own memories, and
his own invisible golden dreams.'" Vivian Paley (1981, pp. 25–26)
records this discussion about *Tico and the Golden Wings*:

> *Teacher:* I don't think it's fair that Tico has to give up his
>   golden wings.
>
> *Lisa:*   It *is* fair. See, he was nicer when he didn't have any
>   wings. They didn't like him when he had gold.

Wally:	He thinks he's better if he has golden wings.
Eddie:	He *is* better.
Jill:	But he's not supposed to be better. The wishingbird was wrong to give him those wings.
Deana:	She *has* to give him his wish. He's the one who shouldn't have asked for golden wings.
Wally:	He could put black wings on top of the golden wings and try to trick them.
Deana:	They'd sneak up and see the gold. He should just give every bird one golden feather and keep one for himself.
Teacher:	Why can't he decide for himself what kind of wings he wants?
Wally:	He *has* to decide to have black wings.

Paley notes that she and the children did not agree about Tico: "I applaud him as a nonconformist while they see him as a threat to the community" (p. 25).

It is interesting to contrast this discussion in a kindergarten classroom with a discussion in a third-grade classroom after the students had heard *Tico and the Golden Wings* as part of a study of traditional and modern fables. These third graders sympathized with Tico and were angry with his friends:

> "They [his friends] only seemed to like him when he was helpless! They should have been happy for him when he got those wings."
> "That was so mean to leave him all alone just because the feathers were gold."
> "He wasn't bragging or anything. He was just happy . . . and they made him feel bad."
> "That's not the way friends should be."

Later in this discussion, these third graders focused on the last lines of the story:

> "I think in the end he was happy that his friends were back, but he was also sad."
> "I think he *knew* that his friends just didn't like him to be different . . . and that made him feel bad . . . but, inside, he knew that everyone is really different because of their memories and dreams."
> "And he had really special memories of all the people he helped!"
> "I think the author [Lionni] wanted those last lines to teach a lesson. . . . Like in the old fables, the lessons were added right at the end. . . ."

"Tico liked being special . . . different. . . . And I think Mr. Lionni is just saying *everyone* is different and we should appreciate differences instead of just thinking they're bad."

"But what was really special about Tico was how kind he was and the other birds never even knew what he did. . . ."

"But *Tico* knew! Those were his special memories."

A single text can be the source of multiple interpretations, and each discussion about that text is unique. As students and teachers explore interpretations together, they begin to know each other at a deeper level—as readers, thinkers, and human beings.

Creating a Context for Aesthetic Reading and Literary Discussion

Most literary discussions begin with personal reactions to shared texts. A comfortable, secure, noncompetitive, and nonjudgmental atmosphere allows students to feel free to express themselves and to take risks as they engage in inquiry and discovery and articulate personal responses, interpretations, questions, and opinions. The teacher joins in the group discussion and shares his or her own reactions to the shared text as well as reflections on this aesthetic experience.

Although the literary discussion begins with free response, students need opportunities to learn how to engage in reflection and to take a critical/analytical stance toward a text. The teacher plays a significant role in promoting and supporting the learning involved in reader response. The term *scaffolding* has been used to describe the kind of support a teacher can provide for young readers to help them develop a critical attitude toward literary texts by inviting them to explore multiple meanings and perspectives in these texts, to articulate their ideas and insights, and to support their interpretations and arguments with textual evidence. Trevor Cairney describes scaffolding this way: "I see scaffolding as the behavior of any person that is designed to help another person engage in some aspect of learning beyond their actual level of development" (1996, p. 175). In his discussion of scaffolding, Cairney refers to Rogoff's concept of "guided participation," which is described as a "collaborative process of 'building bridges' from children's present understanding and skills in order to reach new understandings and skills. This, in turn, requires the 'arranging and structuring of children's participation in activities'" (p. 175).

Teachers who engage in scaffolding to support and build on children's transactions with literary texts draw both from a knowledge of children's literature and from an understanding of literary elements and genres and of the *craft of authors and artists* who create literary texts. In their writings about literature study, Maryann Eeds and Ralph Peterson emphasize the importance of teachers' knowing about the literary elements (1995), and they "advocate using the language of literature as a natural part of talking about books" (1997, p. 56). Their work calls attention to the important role of the teacher in literature discussions in which children learn to explore multiple interpretations and build deeper meanings. The teacher can "move talk beyond mere sharing of impressions and reactions toward that deeper level of noticing and insight that we call *dialogue.* It is in these moments of dialogue with others that our understanding and appreciation of literature are deepened" (Eeds & Peterson, 1995, p. 10). See Chapter 5 ("The Art of Questioning") in the present volume for discussion of scaffolding in which the teacher encourages students to move toward inquiry, analysis, and discovery through questions and "invitations" that stretch their minds and imaginations.

For example, in *The Wreck of the Zephyr* (1983), Chris Van Allsburg uses the story-within-a-story device to explain the mystery of a small wrecked sailboat that is on the edge of some cliffs high above the sea. The fourth-grade students featured in Chapter 1 of this book responded to Van Allsburg's story with personal thoughts as it unfolded and at its conclusion. Then the teacher invited them to "step back" from the story to consider the *craft* of the author. After she helped them identify the story-within-a-story device, the children noted the author's use of a "story pattern" in the embedded story told by the old man to explain the mystery of the sailboat. They turned their attention to the three warnings in the embedded story and noted that the central character ignores each of them:

> "When the old sailor warned the boy not to sail during the storm, I just *knew* he was going to get into trouble as soon as he went anyway. . . ."
>
> "And it was the same when he was warned not to sail over land with those magic sails. . . . You can just predict he's not going to pay attention to the warning!"
>
> "A lot of stories have warnings like that, and you *know* they're going to do it anyway. . . . Like, 'don't open that box' or 'don't go in that room.'"
>
> "But if they *did* obey the warnings, it wouldn't be a very good story. . . . Nothing much would happen."
>
> "I like it when there's a warning. . . . You sort of hope he's going to pay attention to it . . . but when he doesn't, it gets more exciting because you know *something's* going to happen, but you don't know what!"

"The author gives little hints about what's going to happen, so you're *expecting* something!"

"Right! You just expect the boat to crash when he flew over land because of the warning that was hidden in that song about Samuel Blue."

"He had *three* warnings! Remember when the sailor warned the boy not to take the magic sails, but he did anyway. So I *knew* he'd get in trouble, and I really wanted him to go back!"

"I know! Me, too! But maybe authors do that on *purpose* . . . to get you *into* it like that, and to give you clues about what's going to happen."

"I see two patterns—the warning pattern and the pattern of three. He [the author] had three warnings in the story, so you know it's important."

"So that must be the author's craft!"

At this point in the discussion of *The Wreck of the Zephyr*, the teacher introduced a literary term for the technique the students had discovered as they responded to this story: *foreshadowing*. By calling attention to the author's use of this device as part of his craft and by teaching the language of literary analysis, the teacher was building a bridge to new understandings that would become an integral part of students' responses to subsequent literary experiences. For example, when, several months later, this same group of fourth graders was introduced to a retelling of the Greek myth about Daedalus and Icarus, *Wings* (Jane Yolen, 1991), their responses revealed that they had internalized this literary concept. When the last line of the prologue about Daedalus was read aloud, "The gods always punish such a man," the children immediately identified this as a foreshadowing of what would happen to Daedalus by the end of the story. Later, when Daedalus warns his son not to fly too high or too low, they again noted that this was a form of foreshadowing and predicted that Icarus would not pay attention to the warnings and would suffer the consequences. In their comments about this ancient myth, many children referred to *The Wreck of the Zephyr*, recalling the warnings that served as foreshadowing and the boy who ignored these warnings.

Teachers who engage in scaffolding also draw from their knowledge of the nature of readers' transactions with literary texts and the *strategies* readers use to construct meaning. Reading research carried out over the past twenty-five years has highlighted the active role of readers in generating meaning by bringing their prior knowledge and experience to the text. Frank Smith introduced the term *nonvisual information* to refer to this prior knowledge used to construct meaning (1978, p. 5). According to Smith, "The meaning that readers comprehend from text is always relative to what they already know and to what they want to know" (1988, p. 154). He refers to organized knowledge or cognitive structures as "the theory of the world in our heads" which enables readers to make predictions as they interact with a text (1988, p. 7): "Prediction means asking questions, and comprehension means being able to get some of the questions answered. . . . There is a *flow* to comprehension, with new questions constantly being generated from the answers being sought" (1988, p. 19). Students are encouraged to use strategies of questioning and prediction to guide the reading-thinking process during their transactions with literary texts. Exposure to high-quality literature and involvement in literary discussions provide opportunities for students to revise and expand *the theory of the world in their heads* and to build new cognitive structures to bring to and enhance subsequent reading experiences.

Judith Langer's view of reading as a meaning-making process involving *envisionment building* was introduced in Chapter 1:

> I use the term *envisionment* to refer to the understanding a reader has about a text. . . . Envisionments develop as the reading develops. . . . What readers come away with at the end of the reading, I call the final envisionment. (1990, p. 812)

During read-aloud experiences in the classroom, students are invited to enter into and respond to the unfolding text with questions, predictions, and interpretations. The invitation to "think out loud" offers students opportunities to practice these meaning-making strategies and to become actively involved in *envisionment building* during the oral presentation. Students who internalize these strategies can use them to guide and enrich their transactions with texts as independent readers. Like Smith, Langer recognizes that "there is a *flow* to comprehension" (Smith, 1988, p. 19) and that "envisionments develop as the reading develops" (Langer, 1990, p. 812). According to Langer, this flow of comprehension continues *after* the final envisionment, which is "subject to change with time, as the result of conversations with others, the reading of other works, or pondering and reflection" (1990, p. 812).

Shelby J. Barrentine (1996) uses the term *interactive read-aloud* to describe this ongoing dialogue before, during, and after the presentation of a story to a group.

> Rather than reading the entire story without class feedback, the teacher reads the story interactively. Before and during reading, the teacher elicits predictions, poses questions, and utilizes illustrations. Students respond to the teacher's invitations for discussion and also offer spontaneous comments during the read-aloud

session. After reading, the teacher helps the children to pull together loose ends that remain from the reading discoveries. (p.
52)

Like Vygotsky, who has highlighted verbal interaction with peers and
adults as a critical factor in learning (1978), Barrentine sees dialogue in
interactive read-aloud experiences as an opportunity for children to
learn to generate meaning in response to literary texts: "The reading
conversations help children construct meanings that go beyond what
they could construct alone or without verbal interaction. As talk occurs,
the community of listeners builds a shared meaning for each story"
(1996, p. 53).

Literature Study

A reader's *literary history* is an integral part of the prior knowledge he
or she brings to a text. Teachers support aesthetic reading and literary
discussion by encouraging students to reflect on each new text in light
of prior texts in their literary histories and to use *intertextual links* to
generate meaning. In his discussion of intertextual links, Richard Beach
notes:

> With each new text, readers apply an evolving literary 'data bank'
> of prior literary experiences, learning to 'read resonantly' (Wolf,
> 1988). By learning to conceive of texts as representative of certain
> types of genres . . . or of text aspects in terms of prototypical con-
> cepts ('villain,' 'happy ending,' 'foreboding event,' and so forth),
> readers learn to evoke prior knowledge of related literary experi-
> ences. (1990, p. 70)

In his research on the way readers understand texts, Beach and his colleagues found that "the more stories they [the students in this study]
read, the richer their intertextual links, which, in turn, related to the
quality of their interpretation of the story" (Beach, 1990, p. 70). The results of this study are consistent with other studies of intertextual link-
ing which, taken together, suggest the value of "continually relating
current texts to past texts so that students build a sense of their own
histories as readers" (Wolf, 1988).

In his reporting of a study of the intertextual links made by readers reading multiple texts, Douglas Hartman discusses two features of
intertextuality:

> One is that reading is an orchestrated effort by readers to draw
> upon and link memorial and material[1] textual resources located
> in many places to make sense of passages in relation to each other.

> . . . The other feature of intertextuality as a cognitive construction in the reader is the revising of past textual resources and links by looping current textual resources and links back through prior inner texts. As a result, the reading of multiple passages is the deconstruction and reconstruction of links among textual resources. (1995, p. 556)

In the concluding segments of his report, Hartman explores some of the implications of this study:

> Thus, the results of this study indicate that prior knowledge is not something that readers merely bring to the passage and unload before they read; rather, it is something that is utilized, constructed, and reconstructed by readers throughout reading. Understandings of one passage can influence or color understandings of subsequent or previous passages—implicitly or explicitly— throughout the reading encounter. . . . As many of the students in this study demonstrated, their understandings of one passage spill over into their understandings of other passages—both past and future—such that a reading is always open to further interpretations. (p. 558)

In the context of literary discussions, teachers guide their students to use their understandings of past texts to enrich their understandings of current texts and to use insights from current texts to revise interpretations of past texts. For example, the fourth graders who were introduced to *Wings* were able to draw from their prior experience with *The Wreck of the Zephyr* to respond to this current text, and their transactions with this ancient myth were enriched accordingly. Conversely, the following literary discussion from a first-grade classroom illustrates the way in which insights from a current text can be used to revise interpretations of a past text. After listening to Aesop's "The Ant and the Grasshopper," these first-grade children expressed their approval of the harsh justice pronounced by the ant. Later, this same group was introduced to Leo Lionni's *Frederick* (1967), in which Frederick the mouse did not collect grain with the other mice in preparation for the long winter. Unlike the ant, these hard-working mice tolerated, good-naturedly, Frederick's uniqueness, and his poetry provided them with food for the mind and spirit and imagination during the dark days of winter. After comparing Lionni's story with its ancient counterpart, the children revised their initial interpretation of the ant's response to the grasshopper:

> "That ant was mean to the grasshopper just because he didn't do the same work, but Frederick's family was nice to him. I changed my mind about that ant!"
>
> "Frederick made poems, and the grasshopper made music. But the *mice* knew that Frederick did important work."

"Music is important, too, but the ant didn't think so and just shut the door on the grasshopper so he didn't get any food and I don't think that was right!"

"I think the ant should've said to come in and then they could have food *and* music together like the mice family, and *that* would be a better ending."

Laurence Sipe studied the intertextual connections made by first and second graders during storybook read-alouds. Sipe defined intertextual connections as "talk which links the picture storybook being read to other sources of information or discrete semiotic arrays, such as other books, songs, television, videos, and advertising" (2000, p. 78). His study demonstrated that children use intertextual connections to interpret, analyze, and understand the story being read aloud (pp. 77–78). In his concluding comments, Sipe focuses on the need to create "intertextually rich environments." For example, he notes that the more stories children know, the more they can "understand/interpret richly any given story" (p. 86). In addition, "letting children talk *during* the reading of the story assists them in making intertextual connections at appropriate times and in ways that will scaffold their understanding (and give voice to their creative impulse) in tandem with their experience of the story *as it is experienced*" (p. 86). He also observes that "it is important for the teacher to pursue the spontaneous intertextual connections the children make" (p. 86). It is clear that the teacher plays a key role in supporting and building on children's transactions with literary texts by enabling them to use intertextual connections to extend their literary understanding and to explore multiple interpretations and, in Langer's phrase, "a horizon of possibilities."

In addition to using prediction, questions, and intertextual links to generate meaning, readers use other strategies in their transactions with literary texts, such as making inferences about implicit information. Although writers of children's books provide explicit information to help young readers and listeners make sense of literary texts, these writers also include implicit information that requires readers/listeners to make inferences and to fill in gaps in the narrative. Lea M. McGee (1996) uses the term *gap-filling activities* to describe children's inferential thinking as they move beyond the literal level of understanding toward interpretations of the story as a whole (p. 196). That is, such activities focus on what is *not* in the story and what the active reader must infer about probable missing information.

For example, in an introduction to a third-grade literature unit featuring stories of heroes and heroines, the teacher invited her students to search for clues about characters' qualities, traits, motives, and inner thoughts and feelings. These clues were often quite subtle. One of the stories in this unit was a story from Iceland, "Tritil, Litil, and the Birds," found in a book of troll tales from around the world collected by Ruth Manning-Sanders (1972). As the children listened to this tale, they were especially interested in the giant troll wife. They noted that she did not fit the stereotype of the "villain," and they found clues that revealed the complexity of this character:

"I don't think she's really a villain. . . ."

"But she's mean . . . like when she gave the two brothers impossible jobs and then turned them into slippers . . . and she's a *giant*!"

"But they deserved it. They were so selfish!"

"Later though, you could see she was really nice . . . when she asked Kurt [the youngest of the three brothers] if he had any food and he said he gave it to the birds and she said, 'Those who waste food must go hungry,' but then she gave him that delicious porridge. . . ."

"So it's like her *words* don't match her *actions*!"

"I think the storyteller should *say* if the giant troll is good or bad . . . so you'd *know*!"

"I like it when the story doesn't tell you everything and you have to figure it out from little clues."

"Another clue was when Kurt got help with the jobs and she *knew* he had help and she said, 'I'll let it pass,' like she was sort of glad. . . ."

"When she said, 'Lad, Lad, you're not alone in this,' [p. 30] she didn't say it in a mean way. . . . I think she *knew* he got help because he was kind to those tiny troll guys. . . . Maybe they told her."

"And another good clue was when Kurt went away . . . and a big tear rolled down her face. So you knew she had *feelings* and was just lonely and really liked Kurt. He was so polite and respectful."

"So even though she was a giant troll and you *expect* her to be mean and scary and even though her *words* were mean and scary, her *actions* were nice . . . like J. said before . . . and the tears showed she had a warm heart."

"I think if the story *told* you she's a bad giant or a good giant, then it would be a different story. . . . It wouldn't have any surprises in it."

"My mom always says, 'You can't tell a book by its cover.' . . . You have to get to *know* someone to see if you like them. . . . I think Kurt knew she was nice *inside* even though she was scary to look at. . . ."

"Maybe that's what's important about the story. . . ."
"That could be the *theme* . . . and it's only the hero, the *kind* brother, who finds out that she's not the way she looks!"

It is worth noting the way these third graders collaborated in their search for clues to fill in the gaps in this tale. Their gap-filling inferences enabled them to interpret the story as a whole and to formulate a theme. In the course of their literary discussion, they also reflected on the nature of story and the need for readers and listeners to fill in gaps in order to generate meaning. In her introduction to this literary unit, the teacher engaged in scaffolding by asking the children to *look for clues* about the various characters they would encounter in each of the tales selected for this cumulative literary experience. That is, she provided the children with a framework that helped them "move beyond the literal level of understanding toward interpretations of the story as a whole" (McGee, 1996, p. 196).

By demonstrating a "cover-to-cover" study of literary selections, the teacher can help children discover clues on the front and back covers, the dust jacket, endpapers, front matter such as dedication and title pages, author's notes, and other text or pictures that precede or follow the story text. According to Margaret Higonnet (1990), French critics use the term "peritext" to refer to these peripheral features as well as the illustrations that surround or enclose the verbal narrative in picture books or in illustrated chapter books.

A group of kindergarten children was invited to talk about the pictures on the front and back covers of *That Apple Is Mine!* (Arnold, 2000) after hearing the title of this retelling of a Russian folk tale.

"I see three animals and a big red apple on the front. One's a rabbit and one's a bird."
"One looks like a porcupine. The bird has a necklace on."
"Maybe it's a crow because they like shiny things, and they steal eggs and shiny things. Maybe he stole it. And he's holding the big apple. Maybe he stole it, too."
"But maybe they *all* want it because it says . . . 'That Apple Is Mine!'"
"On the back cover it's a green apple, and there's a little worm peeking out. What's he saying?"

The teacher read the words of the worm printed in a speech balloon: "And this one is mine!" Then she showed the title page and the next two pages preceding the story text, and asked the children, "What do you notice?"

"Look! That crow is stealing the 'P' in the word APPLE!"
"I told you that's what crows do."

> "On the next pages there's leaves falling all over."
> "It must be fall."

The teacher read the first two lines of the story: "The fall was almost over. All the trees were bare except for an apple tree with one last apple on it" (unpaged). Hare wants the apple and asks Crow to get it for him, but Crow flies off with it. Unfortunately, she drops the apple and it falls on Hedgehog. Now they all insist, "That apple is mine!" When Crow drops the apple, the illustration reveals a small worm peeking out of it. Although there is nothing in the text about the worm on this page, the children noticed it immediately:

> "There's the worm that was on the back cover! But now it's in the red apple."
> "It's *in* the apple. So the worm was there first *before* Hare saw it!"
> "I think maybe the apple *really* belongs to the worm!"

As Hare, Crow, and Hedgehog argue loudly over the apple in the next pages, they do not seem to notice the tiny worm. However, the children paid close attention to the worm on each page after having discovered her on the back cover. Although the *text* features Hare, Crow, and Hedgehog fighting over the ownership of the apple, and Bear providing a solution to their conflict, the tiny worm can be found in the *illustration* on each page. The worm is not mentioned in the story text and is so small that she could easily be overlooked. However, the picture on the back cover provided the children with a clue about the importance of this character in the story. The children responded by focusing their attention on the tiny worm throughout the story. Their running comments about the characters as the story unfolded revealed that they identified with the worm rather than with the characters developed in the text. And they used the picture of the worm on the back cover to predict the ending of the story.

When *The Brave Little Parrot*, a Jataka tale from India retold by Rafe Martin (1998), was introduced to a group of second graders, several children observed that the bird on the front cover did not look like a parrot because it was not colorful. However, when the teacher showed them the front flap, illustrated with a single red and green feather, and the title page, with a portrait of a gray-white bird, the children used these "peripheral features" to find clues about the story:

> "Oh, so it *is* a parrot [pointing to the feather on the front flap], but it just doesn't have colors."
> "Maybe this is the kind of story that tells you how the parrot *got* colors!"

> "I get it! Those pictures [pointing to the front cover and title page] show what parrots looked like *before* they got their colorful feathers."

At the end of this story red, green, yellow, and blue feathers grew on the little parrot. However, the text does not describe this transformation as a reward for her selfless and courageous actions that helped save the animals trapped in a raging forest fire. Instead, the storyteller tells of the little parrot's delight that what she had done had somehow saved her friends. The children filled in the words that were not in the text:

> "I think her transformation was a reward for her kindness and courage."
> "But she only did it to save her friends, *not* for a reward."
> "Maybe that's why it [the text] only tells how happy she was that they were okay!"

One child used the language pattern found in the *pourquoi* tales they had heard earlier in the year to add a last line: "So that's why parrots have colorful feathers to this very day!"

The dedication page found at the back of the book includes text presented as "A Note on the Story," and this note prompted further discussion about the meaning of this ancient tale and the lesson it teaches. One child saw a connection between this note and Rafe Martin's dedication: "For my teachers." She commented, "I think he dedicated this book to his teachers because the story teaches a lesson!" The children's cover-to-cover study of this book concluded with a discussion about the significance of the two feathers on the dedication page and the single feather on the back flap.

When *Journey*, Patricia MacLachlan's contemporary novel about abandonment (1991), was introduced in a shared reading experience, the teacher invited the students to discuss the title and to suggest possible meanings. Beneath the title on the front cover of the Delacorte Press edition of the book is a picture of an old camera. The students were asked to consider the possible significance of this object featured alone on the cover. The title page features a segment of a torn photograph revealing a child's arm. This page provides them with a further clue about the significance of photography and photographs in this novel. Two pages prior to Chapter 1, the author includes two quotations that offer additional clues about the meaning of the title and the pictures of the camera and the torn photograph:

> It is our inward journey that leads us through time—forward or back, seldom in a straight line, most often spiraling. (Eudora Welty, *One Writer's Beginnings*)

> Photography is a tool for dealing with things everybody knows about but isn't attending to. (Emmet Gowin, quoted in *On Photography* by Susan Sontag)

The page that immediately precedes Chapter 1 is written in italics and sets the stage for the story. This introductory page, or prologue, opens with these lines: "Mama named me Journey. Journey, as if somehow she wished her restlessness on me. But it was Mama who would be gone the year I was eleven." When his mother tells Journey that she will be back, his grandfather says, "No, son. . . . She won't be back." In response to these words, Journey hits his grandfather. Here, the scene ends.

Thus, prior to hearing the first chapter, students have gained a great deal of information about this story. The title of the book not only refers to an inward journey but also to the name of the protagonist and to his mother's physical journey. The prologue suggests that the story will be told as a first-person account from the viewpoint of Journey and is about his response to being abandoned by his mother, who has left him and his older sister with their grandparents. The prologue also offers clues about Journey's inner conflict. When his grandfather contradicts his mother's words, Journey cannot tolerate this. He prefers to hold onto his own idealized image of his mother (suggested in the prologue) rather than face the harsh reality his grandfather offers him. His denial of this reality and his attack on his grandfather foreshadow the conflict between Journey and his grandfather that is revealed as the story unfolds.

At the conclusion of the story, the students were invited to return to their initial discussion of the text and the pictures that preceded the first chapter. In this follow-up discussion, the "peritext" was used as an important part of their study of the story as a whole. For example, the camera on the front cover was identified as a symbol used to develop a central theme in the story: the search for truth. Journey's search for the truth about his mother and about his past guides his emotional journey. He is able to accept the cold reality of abandonment only when he finally confronts the truth. The torn photograph on the title page was identified as a clue about the breach in the family circle. By the end of the novel, a new family unit is established, bound together by love and caring.

Literary Discussion: The Social Context

Through literary discussion, teachers and students collaborate to study, explore, and respond to literature in a social context. As children share their reading experiences with others and talk about their thoughts, feelings, associations, interpretations, understandings, and questions, they develop a *community of readers*. Susan Hepler and Janet Hickman (1982) used this term to describe children working together to become readers of literature and to explore and build meanings together. Lea McGee expands on this idea: "Children who talk together about books create what Fish (1980) calls an interpretive community—a group of readers who share their idiosyncratic interpretations and negotiate a group-constructed view of a story or poem" (1995, p. 108). In these interpretive communities, participants have opportunities to share their personal responses to the text and to benefit from the insights of others. "Through talking together, children may propose, defend, negotiate, become aware of, and accept multiple interpretations" (McGee, 1995, p. 109).

In her discussion of an extended study of reading and writing in classroom settings, Jane Hansen (1987) highlighted the central role of "community" as a context for learning. In the classrooms she observed, readers and writers supported and learned from each other and, in the process, learned *about* each other. "We start with this assumption: everyone knows something others will find interesting. Background knowledge, important for comprehension, differs for all. . . . [A] community is composed of individuals, each of whom has a unique contribution to make. The supportive community begins with the teacher's belief that each child has something to share" (pp. 58–59). Hansen also noted that diversity played a significant role in these classroom communities:

> As teachers, we learn to foster diversity because diverse thinking promotes challenges that push our students' and our own learning. . . . In a classroom where students have diverse skills, abilities, and interests, there are many opportunities for the children to learn from and help each other. As teachers, we teach the children to expect, appreciate, and benefit from differences. (p. 59)

In her introductory chapter for *Lively Discussions! Fostering Engaged Reading* (1996), co-editor Janice Almasi shares her view of discussion as a "forum for collaboratively constructing meaning and for sharing responses" (p. 2). When literary discussion occurs in a community of readers who engage in fluid transactions with literary texts and whose initial envisionments change in response to new information in the text, the interpretation that each reader brings to the discussion may be transformed and shaped by the ideas brought by other participants (pp. 2–3). Thus, the reader's interpretation constantly evolves in the course of transactions with the text and interactions with others. Almasi asked students involved in these authentic discussions to define their purpose. "These students' definitions suggest a collaborative environment in which the goal of the event is to share viewpoints, provide a rational argument, and work together to come to new understandings about literature" (p. 3).

Teaching Literature and Literary Discussion

Since Rosenblatt's introduction of the transactional theory of reading in 1938, there has been an ongoing exploration of literary experience and reader response among literary theorists and educational researchers. And, among educational practitioners, there has been a growing interest in translating literary theory and research into the elementary school curriculum. As a result, more students are being exposed to high-quality literature written for children and adolescents and are being introduced to learning strategies to enhance their transactions with literary texts. At the core of the teaching of literature in the classroom is literary discussion of shared texts.

In a review of Rosenblatt's *Literature as Exploration*, Robert Probst (1990) discusses her principles for teaching literature. Rosenblatt's first principle, that "students must be free to deal with their own reactions to the text" (Rosenblatt, 1976, p. 66), is reflected in the current practice of elementary school teachers who support the view of literary discussion presented in this book. They encourage their students to reflect on their own experiences of a text and to articulate the thoughts, feelings, images, and associations evoked by their transactions with the unfolding text.

Rosenblatt's second principle, that "the classroom situation and the relationship with the teacher should create a feeling of security" (Rosenblatt, 1976, p. 66), focuses on the type of environment that supports students who engage in inquiry and reflection and who share personal thoughts, feelings, insights, and interpretations in the context of literary discussion. The teacher who joins in the literary discussion as a partner in the collaborative process of meaning making can model humane and supportive responses to risk-taking behavior.

Another principle for teaching literature suggested by Rosenblatt highlights the social context in which literary discussion occurs: the teacher must try to "find points of contact among the opinions of students" (Rosenblatt, 1976, p. 71). Students are encouraged to identify and explore the similarities and differences in the meanings they generate in response to a shared text as a starting point for discussing values, beliefs, and experiences.

A fourth principle of instruction speaks to the dual function of literary discussion: "Although free response is necessary, it is not sufficient; students must still be led to reflection and analysis" (p. 75). The teacher's challenge is to support spontaneity and personal response *and* to promote and guide reflection and analysis as students engage in collaborative construction of meaning in response to shared texts.

Children's Books Cited

Aesop. (1947). "The Ant and the Grasshopper." In *Aesop's Fables*, illustrated by Fritz Kredel. New York: Grosset and Dunlap.

Arnold, Katya, reteller and illustrator. (2000). *That Apple Is Mine!* Based on a story by Vladimir Suteev. New York: Holiday House.

Korschunow, Irina. (1984). *The Foundling Fox.* Illustrated by Reinhard Michl. Translated by James Skofield. New York: Harper & Row.

Lionni, Leo. (1964). *Tico and the Golden Wings.* New York: Pantheon.

Lionni, Leo. (1967). *Frederick.* New York: Pantheon.

MacLachlan, Patricia. (1991). *Journey.* New York: Delacorte.

Manning-Sanders, Ruth. (1972). "Tritil, Litil, and the Birds." In Ruth Manning-Sanders (collector), *A Book of Ogres and Trolls* (pp. 20–31). Illustrated by Robin Jacques. New York: E. P. Dutton.

Martin, Rafe, reteller. (1998). *The Brave Little Parrot.* Illustrated by Susan Gaber. New York: Putnam.

Van Allsburg, Chris. (1983). *The Wreck of the Zephyr.* New York: Viking.

Yolen, Jane. (1991). *Wings.* Illustrated by Dennis Nolan. San Diego: Harcourt Brace Jovanovich.

3 The Teacher as Reader and Student of Literature

"Reading and discussing . . . books is one way of humanizing our children. I am not so naive as to think literature will save the world, but I do believe it is one of the things that makes this world worth saving."

Charlotte Huck, "I Give You the End of a Golden String"

The Value of Literature

Elementary school teachers who want to create rich literary experiences in which they read and discuss books with their students often ask, "How do I get started?" My initial response to this question is, "Why? Why do you think it is important to include literature in your curriculum and to support literary discussions in which teachers and children construct meaning together?" Preparation to teach any subject to children should begin with an understanding of its inherent value. This is especially true for the elementary school teacher who wants to develop a literature program, since this has not always enjoyed wide acceptance as an integral part of the elementary school curriculum. Charlotte Huck is well known as a remarkable teacher's teacher who has instilled a love of literature in thousands of teachers who have, in turn, brought literature into their own classrooms. During her long career as professor, scholar, and researcher, Huck has called attention to the importance of literature in the lives of children and has played a major role in making a place for literature in the elementary school curriculum. Thus, it seemed fitting to introduce this chapter with her words.

In recent years, many other educators and students of children's literature have articulated their own perspectives about the inherent value of literature and its effect on children's development. In her book *Envisioning Literature: Literary Understanding and Literature Instruction,* Judith Langer writes:

> All literature—the stories we read as well as those we tell—provides us with a way to imagine human potential. In its best sense, literature is intellectually provocative as well as humanizing, allowing us to use various angles of vision to examine thoughts, beliefs, and actions. (1995, p. 5)

According to Janet Hickman and Bernice Cullinan, editors of *Children's Literature in the Classroom: Weaving Charlotte's Web,* most teachers who

weave literature into their total curriculum generally share beliefs about
the inherent values of literature. Hickman and Cullinan begin their survey of these values with a focus on the aesthetic and personal values of
literature: "Good children's books are a form of art and like all art have
an infinite capacity to delight and move us, to touch the emotions and
perceptions that make us truly human" (1989, p. 4).

Excerpts from a literary discussion in a third-grade classroom illustrate the role of literature in the development of new insights about
human behavior. The teacher had introduced these third graders to
folktales from around the world and invited them to identify literary
patterns that crossed cultural boundaries. For example, one group of
folktales featured "opposing characters" or characters with contrasting
traits. The children discovered that some of the storytellers created opposing characters whose deeds were similar but whose motives were
different. In *The Five Sparrows* (Newton, 1982), an adaptation of an old
Japanese tale, an old woman cares for an injured sparrow out of kindness and humane motives and is richly rewarded for her kind deed. Her
neighbor, motivated by jealousy and greed when she sees these rich
rewards, throws stones at four sparrows and then nurses their injuries
just as the old woman had nursed the sparrow she had taken into her
care. Some of the children's responses to this story are included below:

> "The two neighbors are the same. . . . They both took care of spar-
> rows."
> "But they're not *really* the same. . . . The first old woman took
> care of the bird because she *cared* about it and felt sorry for it."
> "She got rich for being kind, but she didn't *do* it to *get* a re-
> ward."
> "Hmmmm . . . that's a *big* difference. The second old woman
> wanted to do the same thing . . . but she just wanted to get rich
> and get respect from her family. . . . She didn't care about the
> birds!"
> "It's like in *The Talking Eggs* [a folktale from the American South
> retold by Robert D. San Souci, 1989]. One sister was really nice to
> the old lady and kept her promise . . . and she got rewarded but
> that wasn't *why* she did it. . . . But the other sister was *only* think-
> ing of *getting* stuff."
> "So the *deeds* are the same, but the *reasons* are different . . . like
> being selfish and greedy."
> "That was awful when she hit the birds. . . . I got so mad at
> her."
> "I think her greed made her cruel."
> "I was glad when she was punished, but I don't get why was
> her whole family punished, too."
> "Because, remember? . . . They were the ones who got her

started thinking about it. . . . *They* were envious and wanted to be rich, too. So they were like *accomplices* in the crime!"

"If she had just gotten someone *else* to hit the birds, then she would have cured them and gotten a reward just like the first lady. . . ."

"Like she could have gotten those boys to do it . . . the ones that hit that first sparrow. . . ."

"NO! I don't think that's right! She *still* did it for a bad reason. She's still selfish and mean, and she never even cared about the birds. . . . So *inside* she's different from the first lady. I think *that's* what's important!"

"I know. It's the *feelings* that're important. Like sometimes I do something nice for my mom . . . because I *want* something. . . . But, it's better to do it just to be helpful. . . ."

"I get it. It's like in *Papa Gatto* [an Italian tale retold by Ruth Sanderson, 1995]. . . . Sophia went to take care of Papa Gatto's kittens because she wanted the diamond bracelet . . . but the stepsister did it because she really loved the kittens!"

In each of these folktales featuring "opposing characters," greed and cruelty provide a contrasting background to highlight humane behavior. The children absorbed the wisdom of these ancient tales from diverse cultures as they probed beneath the surface behaviors to discover the inner motives that provided the basis for judging between good and evil. Through this type of literary discussion, children discovered story patterns representing universal truths that cross cultural boundaries, and they worked together to build understandings about the nature of human experience.

Hickman and Cullinan highlight other values of literature in the lives of children. Literature expands the child's world, opening doors to new experiences and knowledge, to diverse cultures, to different lives and ways of living, and to the past. As children enter into the lives of characters in books and explore diverse viewpoints, beliefs, emotions, motives, behaviors, and relationships, they develop new understandings about themselves and others. Literature opens doors to the beauty of nature and art and to our literary heritage. Literature has the power to stretch the mind and imagination and to provide children with material for dreams and ideals. Children draw from the rich language of literature to express their thoughts, emotions, and experiences.

For over thirty years, studies of the relationship between literary and literacy learning have yielded impressive evidence that positive and meaningful experiences with literature play a critical role in the development of literacy skills and contribute significantly to the quality of children's experiences as readers and writers. The research of Dolores Durkin (1961), Robert Thorndike (1973), Margaret Clark (1976), Gordon

Wells (1986) and others revealed that reading aloud to young children contributed directly to their early literacy development. As children move beyond early literacy experiences and read (or listen to) a variety of rich and complex materials, they benefit from the range of linguistic inputs that is unavailable to the nonliterary child (Chomsky, 1972, p. 23). Children who have opportunities to read widely and deeply on a regular basis gain competence and confidence as readers. Through rich and enjoyable literary experiences, students discover that reading can be personally satisfying and that literature addresses their own needs, interests, and questions. In the context of a rich literary environment, children are inspired to become readers who are completely absorbed in their books and who choose to read for pleasure and personal growth.

Developing Rich Literary Experiences in the Classroom

Teachers who want to develop rich literary experiences for their students can begin by learning about the rich diversity of literature available for children. Teachers who know literature can draw from their knowledge to select books that will be appropriate and meaningful for their students and will meet their individual needs and interests. They can select books that foster delight and wonder and stretch their students' minds and imaginations and touch their hearts. They can select books that invite reader engagement, evoke multiple interpretations, and provide opportunities for collaborative construction of meaning in the social context of the classroom. They can select books that offer opportunities for children to learn *about* literature by exploring diverse genres, narrative components, and the craft of authors and artists who create the books they hear and read.

Knowledge of children's literature enables teachers to select literary texts that have multiple layers of meaning and significant truths about the human experience and that challenge students to explore new understandings, interpretations, and insights as they discuss shared literary experiences. The third-grade students who discussed folktales with opposing characters had been introduced to a wide variety of folktales from different countries so they could *discover for themselves* recurring patterns that reflect important truths about human nature. Their teacher drew from her knowledge of folklore in general and her awareness of specific illustrated retellings of tales featuring some of these recurring patterns to plan rich, cumulative literary experiences. These experiences provided the background knowledge the children used in their collaborative construction of meaning in response to shared texts.

The construction of meaning in response to literary texts is learned. Teachers can promote and support this learning by drawing from their knowledge of the strategies used by proficient readers in their transactions with literary texts as well as the tools of literary analysis used by critical readers. In her preface to *A Critical Handbook of Children's Literature*, Rebecca Lukens writes: "Learning to recognize such literary elements as character and plot and theme helps us understand the effects a writer achieves and appreciate the reasons for his or her choices" (1999, p. xii). Knowledge of literary genres, narrative elements, and the craft of authors and artists enhances readers' appreciation and enjoyment of literature and enables them to explore literary texts with a critical eye.

For example, the third graders who had been introduced to stories with opposing characters learned to recognize this recurring literary pattern. Further exploration of the craft of the storytellers who chose to build their stories around opposing characters was prompted by one child's question: "But why do these stories need to have *both* of these characters that are so much alike?"

> "They're not *really* the same. They're different."
> "One's good and one's bad. They're opposite! But they're *also* alike. . . . Like they can be sisters or neighbors or even twins."
> "I think the storyteller decides to have a mean one to make the good one look *really* good . . . in comparison."
> "Oh, I get it . . . and the mean one gets punished and the good one gets rewarded . . . so that's the *whole* pattern. . . ."

In her glossary of literary terms, Lukens defines the *character foil* as "a character whose contrasting traits point up those of the central character" (1999, p. 336). These third graders worked together to articulate their own understanding of the role of the character foil in the pair of opposing characters in each story. This term, "opposing characters," became an integral part of their literary vocabulary and enriched their responses to subsequent texts. For example, several months after their initial exposure to opposing characters, this group was involved in a study of variants of the Cinderella tale. When *Mufaro's Beautiful Daughters: An African Tale* (Steptoe, 1987) was introduced, the children were asked to talk about the two sisters on the front and back covers. They used clues on the covers to identify the sisters as "opposing characters":

> "You can tell they're different. . . . One sister is vain. . . . She just thinks she's so great. . . . She's looking in the mirror . . . with her face like this [imitates the body language and facial expression of the girl on the front cover]. But the other one on the back is working in the field. . . . She's a hard worker."

> "And she has animals and birds around her so it shows she's kind to nature."
>
> "The one on the front has a sneaky look."

As the story unfolded, the children continued their focus on these opposing characters and were able to confirm their initial comments:

> "And she really *was* sneaky. . . . The way she talked behind her father's back was so mean . . . but she was always so-o-o sweet when he was around!"
>
> "And Nyasha *was* kind to nature. . . . She was kind to that little snake."
>
> "Manyara was really mean to her sister and that little boy and the old lady. . . . She thought she was better than everyone . . . just like on the cover. . . ."
>
> "When Manyara came, the boy had to *beg* for food, but she refused. . . . But when Nyasha came, she just *gave* him food because she saw he was hungry."
>
> "I *knew* she would do that . . . because the other one didn't!"
>
> "That's the thing about opposing characters. . . . If the bad one does something mean, you can just predict that the other one will do something kind."
>
> "And the bad one makes the other one look even better."
>
> "He's such a good artist [Steptoe]. It's like you can walk into the pictures, they're so real. And all those birds and flowers. . . . But he only puts them around Nyasha. . . . Even on the cover. . . . See, they're *only* around her. . . . That's another clue about the opposing characters."

This observation prompted the teacher and children to examine each page again to confirm its validity. They concluded that the author/artist must have deliberately created the pictures to call attention to the significant differences between the two sisters. Since it was a student who had made this interesting discovery (not the teacher), it was he who led his classmates and teacher in an exploration of Steptoe's craft as an artist and the way he created meaning through an interdependence of text and illustrations.

Teachers who see themselves as partners with their students as they journey together through the world of literature are able to encourage and support these student-initiated explorations and discoveries and grow *with* their students. Literary discussions evolve as teachers and students together embark on a quest for understanding, explore possibilities, and engage in collaborative construction of meaning in response to shared literary texts. The teacher's responsibility is to create a safe environment in which students can share personal responses to literary texts and take risks as they articulate interpretations and explore uncharted realms of ideas. Students need to know that their responses will be honored. At the same time, teachers can help children build an awareness of literary elements and genre and the craft of authors and artists by exposing them to a wide range of quality literature and demonstrating ways to use this literary knowledge to enrich their transactions with literary texts. Drawing from their years of observations of literature studies, Maryann Eeds and Ralph Peterson share their conclusions about why it is important for teachers to help students develop literary awareness:

> We have learned that a gradual increase in awareness of how various authors use literary elements within particular stories enables readers to enter even further into a story world and greatly enrich their reading experiences. And we believe that awareness of literary elements and of their function in a story nurtures the development of children's ability (and our own) to respond imaginatively to a text, opening the way to dialogue and providing insight into layers of story meaning that may otherwise go unremarked. (1995, pp. 10–11)

The Teacher as Reader and Student of Literature

Many teachers who explore literature with their students also engage in literary explorations on their own as readers and students of literature. There are many excellent professional resources available to guide teachers in their personal journey through the world of children's literature. (A list of resources for teachers can be found in Appendix A.) A teacher's personal journey can also be enriched through interactions with colleagues in his or her school or district. In the school where the author teaches, one of the faculty study groups established to promote professional development features the study of recent publications in children's literature. The participants read, recommend, and discuss selections in after-school sessions scheduled during the second semester. "Book talk" among colleagues, however, extends beyond these scheduled meetings and continues as an integral part of the ongoing dialogue in which teachers engage in inquiry and discovery as perpetual learners and share ideas for developing literary experiences for their students. In the context of this community of readers, teachers also enjoy discussing adult literature, and favorite titles are brought to school so others can enjoy them.

Teachers who read and study literature for their own pleasure and growth can build the knowledge and attitudes necessary to develop rich literary experiences for and with their students. They view themselves as partners in the quest for understanding and grow with their students as they journey from the known to the unknown together.

Students who have opportunities to share the joys of literature with teachers who love to read and who are themselves students of literature are indeed fortunate! These teachers are prepared to help their students learn how to read literature and, at the same time, they are ready to experience literature along with their students as they explore this treasure-house of ideas and language together. As Hickman and Cullinan (1989, p. 10) have observed:

> An enthusiastic teacher who reads and enjoys books, shares favorites, asks for recommendations, and joins the class in solving legitimate questions about their common reading becomes a point of focus for students, some of whom may have no other model for fully literate behavior.

Children's Books Cited

Newton, Patricia Montgomery, adapter. (1982). *The Five Sparrows: A Japanese Folktale*. New York: Atheneum.

Sanderson, Ruth, reteller. (1995). *Papa Gatto: An Italian Fairy Tale*. Boston: Little, Brown.

San Souci, Robert D., reteller. (1989). *The Talking Eggs: A Folktale from the American South*. Illustrated by Jerry Pinkney. New York: Dial.

Steptoe, John, reteller. (1987). *Mufaro's Beautiful Daughters: An African Tale*. New York: Lothrop, Lee & Shepard.

4 Selecting Books to Read Aloud

Selecting Books That Foster Lively Discussions

Lively literary discussions often arise in response to literary texts that challenge students to build new understandings and insights as they explore layers of meaning, consider new perspectives, and confront difficult issues in collaboration with their classmates. The quality of literary discussion depends, in large part, on the quality of the literary texts selected for sharing in a group experience. Books that offer multiple layers of meaning and significant truths about the human experience stimulate students to stretch their minds and imaginations as they move toward deeper levels of understanding, appreciation, interpretation, and insight. Teachers who introduce their students to diverse literary genres and fine authors and artists help them develop a literary and artistic awareness that will enrich their transactions with literary texts and, in turn, their contributions to discussions of these aesthetic experiences.

The picture book *The Lion and the Mouse,* by Carol Jones (1997), was read aloud to a group of first graders as one of a series of thematically related stories. The children compared this modern version with the traditional Aesop's fable and identified Jones's revisions. (The bibliography at the end of this chapter includes five illustrated retellings of Aesop's fable "The Lion and the Mouse.") They noted the additional characters and the new setting in Jones's text, and they identified the new conflicts added to the plot. The final page of this picture book shows separate portraits of the lion and the mouse linked together with the words: "One good deed deserves another." Most of the children had little difficulty applying this moral to the deeds of the lion and the mouse and connecting this theme to examples of reciprocity in their own lives. The discussion became more lively when one child observed: "In *this* story [Jones's revision], the lion and mouse were not the *only* characters who did good deeds." This comment prompted the other children to return to the text to search for the less obvious examples of lifesaving deeds. They found that Monkey had saved Mouse from Crocodile's jaws and that, later, Mouse was able to save himself from Python by using the aerial skills he had learned from Monkey. However, after a careful review of the text and detailed illustrations, they concluded that

Mouse had never repaid Monkey for what he had done for him. Excerpts from the discussion that followed this discovery reveal the children's thoughtful involvement in this literary analysis:

> "I think she [the author] should've ended it better so the Monkey could get a reward, too."
>
> "But this story is more like real life because it doesn't always work like that."
>
> "I know. You don't *always* get something you deserve."
>
> "But you shouldn't just do a good deed so you'll get a reward. I think Monkey was just being friendly."
>
> "My mom says when you do something good, the reward is that you *feel* good inside!"
>
> "Maybe Monkey felt happy inside because he helped somebody in trouble!"
>
> "My mom says that, too! You shouldn't *expect* anything in return, but if someone does something for you, you *should* try to do something nice back."
>
> "I think Mouse probably wanted to. Remember in this one part . . . [locates the relevant scene in the narrative] he tried to go back to Monkey?"
>
> "We could write a 'to be continued' story! Mouse could come back later to see Monkey in the jungle with his brothers and sisters and they could all get to be friends with Monkey. . . ."
>
> "And with Lion, too! He and Mouse were *friends* at the end. See . . . it even shows it in the last picture. . . . See how their tails are curled around each other? Remember . . . we learned the sign language for 'friend'? See? [Here, the student demonstrated the sign for friendship.] It's just the same!"
>
> "I think the artist must know sign language! So, we *should* put the lion in our story, too . . . and they can *all* be friends together."

Following this discussion, the children reinforced their notion of reciprocity with the creation of their own sequel or "to be continued" story.

In subsequent sessions, these children continued their exploration of this literary theme as they responded to related texts: Mark Ezra's *The Hungry Otter* (1996), a story about the reciprocity between an otter and a crow; Bill Peet's *The Ant and the Elephant* (1972), in which a grateful ant rescues his rescuer, a huge elephant; Joanne Oppenheim's adaptation of a Grimm tale in *One Gift Deserves Another* (1992); and *The Mean Hyena: A Folktale from Malawi*, retold by Judy Sierra (1997). Sierra concludes this tale of revenge with these words from the storyteller within the story: "So, you see, don't play a trick on someone unless you want an even bigger trick played on you." One child responded, "It sounds just like the other stories! You could say 'One mean trick deserves another.'" A second child added, "What the storyteller said is sort of like the Golden Rule." An explanation of this interesting observation sparked further discussion.

Almost six months after these selections were read aloud and compared, the teacher introduced this group of first graders to *The Full Belly Bowl,* a modern fantasy by Jim Aylesworth (1999). As the children listened to the beginning of this humorous story in which an old man does a good deed and, in return, receives a magic bowl that reproduces whatever is put into it, their eyes lit up with recognition. Several children responded together: "One good deed deserves another!" They were quite pleased to be able to make this intertextual link with the stories they had explored months earlier. The children responded with delight to the humor of these traditional and modern tales that also challenged them to draw from their literary and experiential knowledge to explore layers of meaning in cumulative, collaborative, and animated literary discussions.

After these children had progressed to the second grade, they drew from their literary experiences in the first grade to respond to stories such as *Sirko and the Wolf: A Ukrainian Tale* (Kimmel, 1997) and *The Wolfhound* (Franklin, 1996). As soon as the children discovered the thread of reciprocity running through each of these stories, they made the intertextual link with the stories they had read a year earlier. At the end of each story, several children chanted, "One good deed deserves another!" and then identified the "good deeds" of each character as well as the motives behind the deeds.

Selecting Books That Promote Inferential Thinking

Introducing children to books that challenge them to engage in *inferential thinking* invites them to move beyond the literal level of understanding toward deeper interpretations of each story as a whole. Lea McGee (1996, p. 196) uses the term "gap-filling inferences" to refer to the reader's construction of information or meaning that is implied in the text but is not stated explicitly. That is, writers leave gaps in literary texts, and readers need to fill in these gaps in order to make sense of the text and to understand the literary work as a whole.

For example, in her story "The Hundredth Dove," Jane Yolen (1980) did not state explicitly that the queen-to-be was *also* one of the hundred doves the fowler was pursuing for the king's wedding feast in response to the king's command. After listening to this modern fairy tale, a group of fourth graders discussed the clues they had identified as the story unfolded in order to fill in this significant gap in the text.

They drew from their prior experiences with transformation tales to make the inferences necessary to understand the fowler's terrible dilemma and his own inner transformation at the end of the story.

A group of first graders was introduced to *The Glass Mountain*, a Grimm tale retold and illustrated by Nonny Hogrogian (1985), and *The Seven Ravens*, a Grimm tale adapted by Laura Geringer and illustrated by Edward Gazsi (1994), and asked to compare these two traditional tales. The children engaged in a comparative analysis that reflected their inferential thinking as they "filled in the gaps" to make sense of these stories:

> "The queen [in *The Glass Mountain*] wanted peace and quiet because her baby was crying and crying so she wished the baby would be a raven and fly away, but she didn't really *mean* it. And it was just the same in the other story [*The Seven Ravens*]. . . . The father got mad at the brothers for making so much noise and wished they'd turn into ravens and fly away."
>
> "So in both stories, they made wishes that they didn't *really* want to come true."
>
> "But the storyteller doesn't *tell* you that. . . . You just have to figure it out."
>
> "I'm sure the queen really loved her baby, but she was so tired and annoyed, she just said it without thinking. My baby brother cries all night, and my mom gets tired and annoyed like that."
>
> "The other story [*The Seven Ravens*] was different, though. The father made a wish he didn't mean, but for a different *reason*. He was so worried about their sick baby . . . and he wanted the brothers to be quiet so the baby could sleep and get better."
>
> "And he felt horrible when his wish came true. . . . Remember how *sad* he was in the story? You don't see the queen again after *her* wish came true, but she probably felt horrible, too!"
>
> "I know. When I get mad at my sister, I always say stuff I don't mean, and afterwards, I feel awful."
>
> "Another thing that was the same was the storytellers didn't tell you *who* made those wishes come true. In *The Glass Mountain* there were clues that it could be that witch-lady in the forest that did it, but the other story didn't have clues like that."
>
> "But it was probably an evil witch or a sorcerer that heard the wish and made it come true! The old stories had people with magic powers, and they did bad stuff like that."

This comparative analysis of two traditional tales demonstrated the children's ability to use their personal and literary experiences to make inferences about information that was not explicitly stated in the texts. Later, these children drew from their analysis of these two Grimm tales to respond to *The Canary Prince* (Nones, 1991), an Italian folktale about a princess who is locked in a tower and a prince who discovers her one day when he happens to pass the castle in the woods. They spend many days looking at each other from a distance, longing to be together. A witch sees them and says to the prince, "You should be together." The prince replies, "Indeed, you are right. But I fear she cannot leave her room, and alas, I have no wings" (unpaged). Shortly after the prince's encounter with the witch, a mysterious book appears in the tower room, and the princess discovers its power to transform the prince into a canary so he can fly up to her room and then to change him back to his human form. At this point in the story, the children immediately made the connection between the witch and the appearance of the magical book, and they responded in terms of the two Grimm tales:

> "It's just like the others. He wished he had wings so he could fly to the princess, and that witch made the wish come true."
>
> "But he didn't exactly make a wish, but the witch knew he wanted wings."
>
> "So she must be a *good* witch because she made the wish come true to *help* him!"
>
> "And in *The Glass Mountain* that witch that made the queen's wish come true was a mean witch. She must've *known* the queen didn't really want her baby to be a raven! She was just being mean."
>
> "There *must* have been a mean witch in the one with the seven ravens. I think that's the best way to explain what the storyteller *didn't* tell about the transformation."
>
> "In this one [*The Canary Prince*] the storyteller doesn't *say* it's the witch who put the book there, and even the princess didn't know how it got there! But I think we could figure it out because of those other stories!"
>
> "But in this story, there's a big clue. Remember when the witch said to the prince, 'You should be together.' I think that shows she wanted to help them get together!"
>
> "So this one had the best clue, and *The Glass Mountain* had a pretty good clue that it was that lady in the forest, but the one with the seven ravens didn't have any clues."
>
> "But that one [*The Seven Ravens*] had a helper and so did this one. In this one it was the good witch who helped the prince get to the tower, and in that one it was the dwarf who helped the girl get to the Glass Mountain to get her brothers to change back to boys!"
>
> "They all *three* had helpers! *The Glass Mountain* had the two giants. They helped the man get to the glass mountain to break the spell!"
>
> "And another thing alike. . . . We thought the giants would be mean, but they were nice, and we thought the witch in this one would be mean and she was nice!"

These three stories had been introduced to this group of first graders as part of a cumulative study of transformation tales. They were complex and interesting enough to stimulate this spontaneous and thoughtful discussion in which the children engaged in inferential thinking to interpret these stories. The children's excitement grew as they discovered new ways to think about these three tales in terms of the literary elements that linked them together.

Selecting Books That Represent Diverse Literary Genres

Children's literary experiences are enriched through exposure to diverse *literary genres*: traditional folktales, fables, myths, and legends; modern fantasy; poetry; contemporary and historical realistic fiction; short stories; biography and autobiography; informational books; and picture books. Experience with different genres enables students to discover the distinguishing features of each genre and to learn what to expect as they listen to or read each genre. In addition, children learn the distinguishing features of traditional and modern literature and the vital relationships between the oral and written traditions. This literary knowledge is a critical factor in children's ability to generate meaning as readers and writers.

For example, a sixth grader who read *Maniac Magee* (Spinelli, 1990) explained why he didn't like it at first: "At first, I started to read it like it was *realism*, but it just didn't seem very believable, so I put it down. But then my friend, Jim, told me it's a tall-tale legend *mixed* with realism, so I read it again, and it's *really* a good book! See, I didn't get it the first time because I didn't see what *kind* of story the author was writing. When you read it you have to know that Maniac is *two* things: he's like a hero in an old legend and he's a regular kid, too." This boy's knowledge of these two distinct genres from the oral and written traditions enabled him to understand this story created by an author who chose to blend two genres to create a memorable book.

Young children who are introduced to *pourquoi* legends often respond with questions such as "Is that really true?" or statements such as "That's not right!" However, after they learn about the nature and origins of legends told by ancient storytellers, these children have the knowledge to make sense of this genre. That is, they no longer *expect* to get information from the legend. Instead, they look for the kinds of questions ancient peoples used to ask about the mysteries of the world and the kinds of stories they created to provide answers to these questions.

Selecting Books That Provide a Context for Learning about Narrative Elements, Discourse Structures, and Author's Craft

Teachers can also plan experiences with books that provide children with opportunities to discover the nature of literary genres as well as *literary elements* (i.e., setting, character, conflict, plot, theme, viewpoint, style, and tone) and relationships among these elements in each narrative. Exposure to a wide variety of literary material gives children opportunities to learn about the basic structures of oral and written discourse: narration, description, exposition, and argumentation. As children study literature, they learn about the tools authors use to create meaning so that, in turn, they can use these tools themselves to generate meaning as they read and write. According to Frank Smith (1984), one learns to write by reading like a writer: the knowledge writers require resides in texts, so reading like a writer helps the student build a background of writer's knowledge (pp. 51–53). Readers use their knowledge of *writer's craft* to make sense of and respond to literary texts. The sixth-grade boy who read *Maniac Magee* was able to apply his knowledge of the author's craft to make sense of this story after his friend called attention to the author's blending of two genres: the tall-tale legend from the oral tradition and the contemporary realism found in modern written literature. The quality of the reading experience depends, to a great extent, on the literary knowledge the reader brings to the process of reading literary texts.

Several kindergarten children were introduced to *Deep in the Forest* (Turkle, 1976), a wordless book about a small bear who comes to the home of three humans—a mother, a father, and a little girl with yellow curls. As the children "read" this story together, they identified its connection to the traditional tale "The Three Bears": "I get it! It's just like 'The Three Bears,' but the author made it the *opposite*!" These children drew from their literary background to create a text for a wordless story and to enjoy the humor of this modern revision.

A group of fourth graders was introduced to *Rumpelstiltskin's Daughter* (Stanley, 1997), a modern revision in which the miller's daughter chooses to marry Rumpelstiltskin instead of the greedy king. Later, their only daughter also refuses to marry this king who is still looking for gold spun from straw. In the end, this clever heroine convinces the king to make her the prime minister instead of his queen. These fourth graders drew from their literary background to enjoy the humorous twists in this modern revision and to reflect on the author's choices as she transformed the traditional tale. Several children checked the copyright date, 1997, to support their conclusion that the author intended this to be a feminist revision:

> "I think the author changed the old tale to make a more modern heroine who is smart and independent and can decide for *herself* who she wants to marry and who can even be a prime minister if she wants!"
>
> "Her mother was the same way!"
>
> "I really like *this* story better than the old one."

Another group of fourth graders was introduced to *The True Story of the Three Little Pigs by A. Wolf* (Scieszka, 1989) during a study of authors' use of *viewpoint* to create stories and elicit reader response. In this modern revision of the traditional tale, Alexander T. Wolf presents his own version of what happened when he encountered the three pigs. These fourth graders immediately identified the way humor was created through a shift in viewpoint. To reinforce their grasp of the role of viewpoint in narrative, the students were asked to create their own "viewpoint revisions" of familiar traditional tales. Thus, this story, along with related selections introduced during this study, served as a context for "reading like writers" and as a springboard for creative writing.

Students who discussed *Maniac Magee* in terms of genre also drew on their knowledge of the "quest pattern" found in traditional and modern literature:

> "This is a quest journey! Maniac goes on a journey to search for a home."
>
> "But there's also another quest. . . . He wants to stop prejudice so people can get along with each other."
>
> "So he has *two* quests, and he's like two people. . . . He's a legendary hero *and* a regular kid. . . ."
>
> "And the *kid* part of him just wants a home and a family, and the *hero* part wants to get rid of prejudice and hatred!"
>
> "And both quests were successful!"
>
> "It [the text] *tells* you he was successful with the prejudice part right away in the preface. . . . Remember after the jump rope rhyme? It says that the girls playing together are from the West End *and* the East End."
>
> "I didn't know what that meant until I found out what the town was like *before* Maniac came. . . . The two sides of the town were completely segregated!"
>
> "It's like the author wants to get you to *go back*—to figure it out."
>
> "He gives clues but you don't *know* they're clues at first."
>
> "I like that kind of story. It makes you think and think."

Selecting Literature That Reflects the Diversity of Our Pluralistic Society

Diversity in the literature introduced to children affirms the pluralism in our society in general and in the classroom community in particular. Diversity in literature gives visibility and voice to underrepresented and marginalized groups and allows children to learn about the heritages and realities of people whose experiences are different from their own. Literature can lead to an awareness of inequities and injustices in history and in our contemporary society. It is important to select literature that challenges negative or distorted images and stereotypes in our society, which are perpetuated in much of the literature available to our children even today. According to Rudine Sims Bishop, the role of multicultural literature

> is ultimately to help "make our world anew," to transform society into one in which social justice and equity prevail . . . [and to serve as] a catalyst for engaging students in critical discussions and for eliciting multiple perspectives and multiple voices in pursuit of understanding. (1997, p. viii)

The works of authors such as Patricia McKissack, Andrea and Brian Pinkney, Mildred Taylor, Virginia Hamilton, Eloise Greenfield, Jacqueline Woodson, Walter Dean Myers, Joseph Bruchac, Laurence Yep, Yoshiko Uchida, Gary Soto, Allen Say, Alma Flor Ada, and Nicholasa Mohr can provide the context for critical discussions in which students confront difficult issues and expand their world views as they encounter the experiences and perspectives of individuals from diverse backgrounds. Judy Moreillon (1999) uses the metaphor of a candle and a mirror to call attention to two dimensions of multicultural literature: "a candle that illuminates the beauty of cultures other than our own [or] a mirror that reflects each person's unique customs and contributions to the fabric of our pluralistic society" (p. 127).

In addition to the ethnic or cultural groups that have traditionally been underrepresented in children's literature, the voices of other groups need to be included in order to introduce children to literature that is truly diverse. For example, there are more and more books that offer the perspectives and experiences of migrants; homeless people; immigrants; children with physical, emotional, mental, and learning differences; children of interracial marriages; foreign children adopted by American parents; and children living in alternative family structures. In addition, there are more and more stories that address issues of gender equity, gender roles, and social class. Finally, if we want our children to think beyond our own pluralistic society and develop a more global perspective, we can select from the international literature that is available for young readers. For example: Beverley Naidoo's *Journey to Jo'burg* (1986) portrays the terrible realities of apartheid from the viewpoint of a thirteen-year-old girl. *Waiting for the Rain* (Sheila Gordon, 1987) is another powerful story set in South Africa when apartheid was a reality. Frances Temple's *Taste of Salt* (1992) takes the middle-grade reader into the lives of those who live in poverty and fear in Haiti. Suzanne Fisher Staples's *Shabanu: Daughter of the Wind* (1989) is set in the Cholistan desert area of modern Pakistan. *The Return* (Levitin, 1987) follows a group of Ethiopian Jews who attempt to escape to Jerusalem. *The Storyteller's Beads* (Kurtz, 1998), another story of this dangerous journey out of Ethiopia in the 1980s, features two girls, one Christian and one Jewish and blind, who develop a friendship that crosses barriers of deep cultural prejudice. Descriptions of Australian culture can be found in books by writers such as Ivan Southall, Colin Thiele, and Ruth Park.

Selection of literature that is truly diverse ensures that *all* children will be able to find themselves and their own experiences in the books offered to them, and they will see themselves as part of the larger human experience. Introducing children to literature that allows them to see themselves in a positive light enables them to affirm their self-worth. At the same time, diversity in literature provides children with opportunities to encounter, understand, and empathize with people who are different from themselves. High-quality literature offers children opportunities to *enter into* unfamiliar worlds created by writers, artists, and storytellers and to walk in the shoes of those whose experiences and perspectives are unknown to them. For example, readers of *My Name is Maria Isabel* (Ada, 1993) are drawn into the life of third grader Maria Isabel, born in Puerto Rico and now living in the United States. As her story unfolds, readers are invited to experience what it feels like to be a new girl who wants to fit in at school. Unfortunately, her teacher does not understand the importance of her cultural heritage for her identity as an individual. *La Mariposa* by Francisco Jiménez (1998) is an illustrated story about Francisco, a young boy who speaks only Spanish and whose father is a migrant worker in California. This story depicts the frustration and isolation experienced by children who do not speak the dominant language. *The Magic Shell* (Mohr, 1995) is a novel about Jaime Ramos, who moves with his family from a quiet village in the Dominican Republic to New York City. He, too, experiences the frustration and loneliness of an "outsider" struggling to adjust to a new culture. *Zlata's Diary: A Child's Life in Sarajevo* (Filipovic, 1994) invites readers to see through the eyes of a young girl whose world is shattered by war at the end of the twentieth century—the war in Bosnia. *Sami and the Time of the Troubles* (Heide & Gilliland, 1992) is a picture book about a Lebanese boy who lives in a time of gunfire and bombs. When the fighting reaches their street, ten-year-old Sami and his family live in a basement shelter. Bombed-out Beirut is Sami's playground. This is the story of a young boy trying to grow up normally in spite of the civil chaos and bombings in war-torn Lebanon.

Selecting Texts That Invite Critical Reading and Discussion

Stories such as *My Name Is Maria Isabel, La Mariposa, The Magic Shell, Zlata's Diary*, and *Sami and the Time of the Troubles* can serve as "catalyst[s] for engaging students in critical discussions" (Bishop, 1997). Two of the criteria that Jerome Harste developed to identify books that are "particularly useful for starting and sustaining critical conversations in classrooms" have been used by this author to select texts that invite critical reading and discussion:

- They show how people can begin to take action on important social issues.
- They help us question why certain groups are positioned as "others." (Harste, 2000, p. 507)

The Royal Bee (Park & Park, 2000) is the story of Song-ho, a poor peasant boy in Korea who is determined to learn how to read and write in spite of the fact that the school admits only the sons of wealthy families. He begins to eavesdrop outside the classroom, listening carefully to the lessons day after day. When winter comes, the teacher allows him to come inside and join the class if he can answer all their questions. He passes this test and earns the respect of the students and their teacher. The following Spring, Song-ho's classmates choose him to represent the school in the Royal Bee, and he is the winner of this yearly contest of knowledge. According to the Authors' Note, "*The Royal Bee* was inspired by the true story of our grandfather, Hong Seung Han, when he was an illiterate boy in late nineteenth-century Korea." This story addresses injustices associated with class differences and offers an example of a single individual, the teacher, who stands up against injustice and offers a young boy a way out of a life of poverty.

Virgie Goes to School with Us Boys (Howard, 2000) is another picture storybook inspired by the childhood stories of the author's grandfather. Set in the South after the Civil War, this is the story of Virgie, a young African American girl who is determined to go to school with her older brothers, who attend a Quaker school for freed slaves. Although her older brother tells her that "girls don't need school," Virgie's father finally agrees to let her go. He tells the children, "All free people need learning—old folk, young folk . . . small girls, too" (unpaged).

The Other Side (Woodson, 2000) is a picture book about Clover, an African American girl who lives on one side of a fence, and Annie, a White girl who lives on the other side. The fence has been there a long time, separating the Black side of town from the White side. One summer these two girls take action against the injustice of this racial barrier. They become friends. As in *Virgie Goes to School with Us Boys*, the historical context is unstated in the narrative, although Howard provides it in an extensive note at the end of *Virgie*. *The Other Side* challenges readers to fill in the gaps left by Woodson and to search for answers to questions triggered by this story of two girls who quietly and peacefully reject racial prejudice. The novel *Maniac Magee* (Spinelli, 1990) also depicts a racially divided town and portrays central characters who work together to break down racial barriers. Both Woodson and Spinelli "show how people can begin to take action on important social issues."

In her autobiography *Through My Eyes* (1999), Ruby Bridges tells the story of her own involvement in the civil rights movement. As a six-year-old child she became a pioneer in school integration, spending her first-grade year as a Black child in a previously all-White school in New Orleans in 1960. *The Story of Ruby Bridges* (1995) is a picture book biography by Robert Coles, a child psychiatrist who portrays Ruby as an inspirational model of courage and faith at an extraordinary moment in American history.

Wings (Myers, 2000) is a thought-provoking story of a boy who is ridiculed for being different. Ikarus Jackson has wings and loves to fly, but the cruelty of others diminishes his joy. One girl stands up to those who see him only as "other" and helps Ikarus find his wings again. On the back flap of this picture book, the author writes about this character: "Ikarus Jackson can fly through the air; I want kids to find their own set of wings and soar with him." The flight theme is also found in *Fly, Eagle, Fly! An African Tale* (Gregorowski, 2000). In his foreword to this adaptation of an old tale, Archbishop Desmond Tutu suggests the analogy to black Africans under apartheid.

Holes (Sachar, 1998) is an inventive blend of adventure, mystery, tall-tale humor, legend, and realism. The central character, Stanley Yelnats, overweight, friendless, a target for bullies, and haunted by a family curse, is wrongly accused of theft and sent to a boys' detention facility. Here, Stanley gains friends and develops physical strength as well as inner strength, wisdom, and a sense of self. He encounters a homeless boy who has been given the nickname Zero by the other inmates, who see him as "other" instead of as an individual. As Stanley gets to know Zero, his perception of him changes, and they develop a special friendship. "Engaging children in conversations about the pernicious effects of 'otherness' can help them begin to see and understand the world in new ways" (Leland & Harste, 2000, p. 5).

Historical fiction and memoirs about the Holocaust include portraits of individuals who made moral choices and acted on them in humane and compassionate ways to make a difference in the lives of others. These individuals took a stand against injustice and evil. Students who read and discuss these texts are challenged to consider the nature and consequences of ancient hatreds and prejudices, of humans' inhumanity to each other, of the heroic actions of single individuals or small groups who have attempted to counter evil unleashed by those in power, and of the triumph of the human spirit in the midst of brutality and dehumanization. For example, *Greater than Angels* (Matas, 1998), a novel based on actual people and events during the German occupation of France, is the story of Le Chambon-sur-Lignon, a tiny village whose citizens decided to protect and care for deported Jewish children. This fictional account is a tribute to real-life heroes, the righteous citizens who risked their lives to save these children and who revealed their courage and humanity in the face of Nazi atrocities and overwhelming evil. *Behind the Bedroom Wall* (Williams, 1996), *Jacob's Rescue* (Drucker and Halperin, 1993) and *Your Name Is Renée: Ruth's Story as a Hidden Child: The Wartime Experiences of Ruth Kapp Hartz* (Cretzmeyer, 1994) also feature non-Jews who risk their own lives to hide Jewish refugees and help them escape from the Nazis.

Some of these stories of courage and compassion have been told in picture storybooks. For example, *The Lily Cupboard* (Oppenheim, 1992) is about Miriam, a young Jewish girl who is hidden in the countryside by strangers who risk their lives to protect her from the Nazis. This story is a tribute to the heroism of the Dutch people during World War II. *Rose Blanche* (Innocenti & Gallaz, 1985) begins as a first-person account of a young girl, Rose Blanche, who describes what she observes when her town comes under Nazi rule. The viewpoint changes to third person in the middle of the story as Rose Blanche becomes personally involved in helping the Jews behind barbed wire. At the end of the story, Rose Blanche, too, becomes a victim. The name "Rose Blanche" was the name of a group of young German university students who protested Hitler's policies and practices. All of the young people in this underground movement were killed. In *Passage to Freedom: The Sugihara Story*

(Mochizuki, 1997), young Hiroki Sugihara's father, the Japanese consul in Lithuania in 1940, disobeys his government and writes visas for thousands of Polish Jews to enable them to escape from the Nazis. *The Butterfly* (Polacco, 2000) is the story of the author's aunt Monique and her great aunt Marcel, who, as part of the French resistance, were among the citizens of France who risked their lives to make their own homes a safe haven for Jews escaping to freedom during the Nazi occupation.

Literature is about life. Transactions with literature that is rich in culturally and historically authentic detail enable readers to enter into the lives of others and to see the world through their eyes and, in the process, to gain insights about human experience. Teachers who are building a literature curriculum can find fiction and nonfiction works that celebrate both diversity and the common bonds of humanity and that offer both candles and mirrors to young readers. They can select literature that helps students discover the kinds of barriers that separate human beings and the nature of prejudice and stereotypes that dehumanize and degrade individuals. They can select literature that exposes students to the heroic actions of those who stand up against injustice and evil and serve as inspirational models of courage and humane behavior. The ultimate goal is for students to move from awareness, understanding, and insight to action. They can begin by looking inside themselves and thinking about the moral choices they can make. They can ask themselves what they can do as individuals to transcend prejudice and to work toward breaking down barriers they see in their own worlds.

Selecting Books That Reveal Significant Truths about the Human Experience

Significant truths or themes about human nature, human relationships, and human experiences are embedded in literary texts. Carefully selected literary texts can set the stage for students to discover these significant truths and to engage in lively discussions as they work together to explore diverse perspectives, insights, and interpretations. Ongoing discussions about the big issues in life—good and evil, love and hate, hope and despair, justice and injustice—enable students to grow beyond the limits of their own personal responses and to expand their understandings and form new insights and perspectives.

The Changing Maze (Snyder, 1985) is a picture storybook about a shepherd boy, Hugh, whose granny had told him an old tale of a wicked wizard-king's magical greenthorn maze and had warned him to beware of this evil place. But one day Hugh is forced to enter this maze to rescue his pet lamb. When he discovers a treasure chest of gold in the depths of the maze, Hugh is faced with a dilemma: he must choose between grasping the gold or leaving it to help his pet lamb. After this story was read aloud to a group of fourth graders, several children identified the segment in the text that reveals this dilemma: "His mind still spun to the golden tune that pulled him back toward the hidden room, except for a secret stubborn part that went on moving his stumbling feet after the sound of the black lamb's bleat" (unpaged). After this segment was reread, the children moved toward an exploration of theme:

> "When he decided to help the lamb, you knew he knew *in his heart* what was important in life."
>
> "That part really shows how *torn* he was . . . like you're pulled in both directions."
>
> "*That's* what a dilemma is. . . . You want both, but you have to choose *one*!"
>
> "I think the theme is don't be greedy."
>
> "Or . . . don't touch anything that doesn't belong to you?"
>
> "I think the theme is that you should help others instead of being greedy."
>
> "Don't let greed overcome you."
>
> "Those rich people who went into the maze were greedy. . . . That's *why* they went into the maze . . . just to get the gold. . . ."
>
> "And Hugh went into the maze to get his pet . . . so the *motivation* is different!"
>
> "So they *all* went into the maze, but for different reasons."
>
> "Hugh loved his lamb, but he really wanted that gold . . . and he and his granny were poor, so it must have been *awful* hard to just leave it."
>
> "But in the end he knew he cared more for the lamb than for the gold."
>
> "In life, love and friendship are more important than gold."
>
> "Love is more powerful than gold, but making the choice is *really* hard."

It is interesting to note the differences in the children's responses as they explored the human dilemma in this story and collaborated in the construction of theme statements. Some children responded in moralistic language; others revealed an awareness of the complexity of life's choices and the blurring of clear-cut dichotomies in real life. Some responses were more specific to the story; others revealed an ability to generalize beyond the story to life in general. The differences in the responses by individual children reflected the wide range of knowledge, experience, and thinking skills represented in this group. However, these children seemed to build on the comments of others to reach new understandings of the big issues in this brief picture book. As a whole, the discussion from which these responses were excerpted reflected the way a single, carefully selected literary text can spark a thoughtful, insightful probing of significant truths about the human condition.

Exploration of internal conflict in picture books such as *The Changing Maze* can prepare students for understanding internal conflicts and dilemmas in novels selected for independent reading. For example, the Newbery award winner *Shiloh* (Naylor, 1991) is the story of eleven-year-old Marty Preston who encounters a young beagle that has run away from his abusive owner. Marty decides to rescue the dog from his brutal master and to keep him hidden from his law-abiding parents. After an intense inner struggle, Marty finally confronts the complex moral dilemma generated by his actions. *Fox in a Trap* (Thomas, 1987) is the story of Daniel, who longs to live an exciting life with his Uncle Pete, a hunter and writer. When his Uncle teaches him how to trap foxes, Daniel finds himself caught between his dream of hunting polar bears and his own deep feelings about living creatures. Many realistic novels intended for students in fourth grade and above feature characters who struggle with internal conflicts or moral dilemmas. These novels stimulate lively discussions as students engage in literary analysis and, in the process, gain insights about themselves as they recognize the confusion, self-doubt, guilt, and inner struggle of the fictional characters.

Selecting Texts That Meet the Diverse Learning Needs and Special Interests of All the Children in the Classroom

In any given classroom there are wide variations among individual children in terms of intellectual, emotional, and experiential readiness to understand literary texts that are read aloud. Children also differ in terms of the reading skills and strategies necessary for them to make sense of texts as independent readers. Thus, all classrooms need to be well stocked with a wide range of age-appropriate, meaningful, and relevant material that meets the needs of students with diverse skills and interests and that fosters personal involvement in shared and independent transactions. That is, the classroom collection would include beginning-reader texts, picture storybooks, wordless books, illustrated "transition" books with more continuous text than beginning-reader books, early chapter books with a few illustrations, and chapter books or novels without illustrations. In addition to introducing children to books that reflect their special interests, it is important to introduce books that expand these interests *and* that open doors to new literary experiences, new possibilities for exploring the world of ideas, and new opportunities for growth and pleasure.

Selecting Thematically Related Texts That Invite Students to Use Intertextual Links to Generate Meaning

Students are invited to search for and identify connections between diverse texts and to learn to use these intertextual links to generate meaning. In the context of cumulative experiences with a series of thematically related texts, students learn to read each new text in light of previous texts. In the process, they discover that one text serves as a preparation for reading subsequent texts and that their own literary history plays a critical role in each new literary experience. For example, the first graders who explored the theme of reciprocity in a series of animal tales demonstrated that they were considering each new text in light of the previous texts introduced in this cumulative literary experience. Their use of intertextual links to explore recurrent themes enriched their responses and the nature of their collaborative construction of meaning.

Another thematic literary unit, developed for fourth- and fifth-grade students, focused on *internal conflicts* of central characters in selected narratives introduced in a series of cumulative group sessions. Cumulative literary experiences provide contexts in which students can learn about the narrative elements of setting, characterization, plot, theme, style, and viewpoint. This particular unit was designed to focus on the nature of internal conflict, an important source of plot in many narratives for younger readers and in most novels for older readers. Thus, the students were introduced to a series of tales featuring characters with internal conflicts or dilemmas. For example, two of the stories mentioned earlier, "The Hundredth Dove," a short story in a collection by Jane Yolen, and *The Changing Maze*, a picture book by Zilpha Snyder, were selected for this thematic unit because the central characters in each story were faced with dilemmas and forced to make difficult choices. In "The Hundredth Dove," the hunter has to choose between obedience to the king and repudiation of the king's command. Will the hunter serve the king in accord with the motto sewn on his tunic or will he free the dove he suspects is, through some enchantment, the king's bride-to-be? The children's discussion of the scene in which the hunter makes the choice led to an exploration of theme grounded in the text:

> "When he decided *not* to let the dove go . . . he made his choice. . . ."
> "And he *knew* it was the wrong choice!"

". . . Because he ripped off that motto on his shirt. . . . *That's* the clue!"

"He *knew* it was the wrong choice because it [the text] says he didn't hunt anymore. . . . He *fed* the birds!"

"He changed because he felt so *bad* about what he did."

"He didn't serve the king anymore. He's serving nature instead."

". . . and he never killed any animals after that either, and he became a vegetarian!"

"You can figure out how he feels inside by what he *does* . . . how he changes."

"The author doesn't *tell* you. But she gives you clues like when he wore her [the dove/queen's] ring on a chain. I think that meant he wanted to always remember what he did."

"He knew he shouldn't obey an order and do something he knew was wrong."

"I think the theme is: You should follow your own heart, not just what others say."

"You should do what *you* think is best instead of just following orders."

"I think the theme is that the right choice isn't always the easiest one."

In another selection for this thematic unit, *The Luminous Pearl: A Chinese Folktale* (Torre, 1990), two brothers go on a quest for a luminous pearl in order to be the one to marry the Dragon King's beautiful daughter. When the youngest brother reaches the Dragon King's treasure house, he is confronted with a difficult choice: he can take only one of two desirable items—a luminous pearl that will enable him to marry the woman he loves, *or* the Golden Dipper he promised to bring to the people in a flooded village he had encountered on his quest-journey.

In *Sophie and the Sidewalk Man* (Tolan, 1992), an early chapter book, Sophie is saving up money to buy a special toy, a hedgehog she hopes will be elected king of Toyland in her school's holiday pageant. However, she is also preoccupied with thoughts of the homeless man she sees each time she walks by the toy store to look at the hedgehog she is eager to buy. In the end, she decides to forego purchasing the toy in time for the pageant, so that, instead, she can give half of the money she has saved to "the sidewalk man." She gives the other half to the owner of the toy store as her first installment on a layaway plan.

Shiloh (Naylor, 1991) and *Fox in a Trap* (Thomas, 1987), both mentioned earlier, are examples of novels that can be included in this study of internal conflict in fictional characters. In the cumulative discussions about these and other stories selected for this unit, the children identified intertextual links that helped them explore the ways diverse authors and storytellers use internal conflict as a central element to create these stories. As they compared the internal conflicts of the central characters in these diverse stories, the students developed deeper understandings of the complexity of each character. In the course of their ongoing dialogue, students gained insights about themselves and their own inner conflicts, as well as about the complexity of human experience in general. The final chapter of this book provides a more extensive description of a thematic literary unit.

Selecting Books That Invite Expressive Engagement

The children whose responses to *The Boy Who Held Back the Sea* (Hort, 1987) were recorded in Chapter 1 became emotionally involved in this story as they entered into the lives of the characters. For example, when the boy in the embedded story "shoot[s] a rock through the schoolhouse window," several children responded immediately with comments such as "Oh no! I can't believe he did that!" Later, when old Captain Blauvelt, believed to have been a pirate, goes into town to tell the guards about the leak in the dike, one of the children whispered, "They're not going to believe you!" The fourth graders who heard Yolen's "The Hundredth Dove" (1980) responded with similar emotion to the terrible dilemma of the central character, Hugh, the high king's fowler. Commanded to bring one hundred doves for the king's wedding feast, Hugh captures ninety-nine doves. By the time the children reached the scene in the story that portrays Hugh's capture of the hundredth dove, they had discovered enough clues in the story to guess that this last dove is actually the queen-to-be who has been mysteriously transformed into a dove. Most of the children had become convinced that Hugh, too, had figured out the true identity of the last dove. However, they also knew that Hugh lived to serve the high king: his motto, *Servo* ("I serve"), was sewn on his tunic over his heart (p. 3). As Hugh struggles with this dilemma, the children responded to him as if they could influence his decision: "Don't hurt her, Hugh!" "You shouldn't!" "I bet he won't." Their shock and horror were evident as they listened to the text: "'*Servo*,' he cried out, his voice shaking. '*Servo*.' He closed his eyes and twisted the dove's neck. Then he touched the motto on his tunic. . . . One quick rip and the motto was torn from his breast" (p. 7). In response to these lines, one child whispered, "Oh Hugh, how could you!" and another sighed, "So he *did* know!"

In a discussion of children's literary responses during read-aloud experiences, Laurence Sipe (2002) identifies a type of expressive engagement in which children talk back to the story or characters (p. 477). According to Sipe, "talking back to the story and addressing characters directly begins to blur the distinction between the story world and the children's world. For a moment the two worlds become superimposed— one transparent over the other" (p. 477). Sipe adds that such responses are evidence of children's deep engagement in the story world and that "they are *deeply pleasurable* for children" (p. 479, italics in the text).

Selecting Books to Read Aloud: Some Criteria

The purpose of this chapter about book selection is to highlight the value of careful selection and to suggest some criteria that could be used in the selection process. Excerpts from actual literary discussions were presented to support and illustrate the thesis stated at the start of the chapter: "The quality of literary discussion depends, in large part, on the quality of the literary texts selected for sharing in a group experience." The following questions were used to guide the selection of the books introduced to the children whose voices are heard in this text:

1. Does this book have the capacity to delight children? Does it foster enjoyment and involvement in the literary experience? Does it invite expressive engagement?

2. Will this book challenge children to stretch their minds and imaginations and will it touch their hearts as they experience the story and respond to this literary experience in a group setting?

3. Will this book foster lively discussion as children engage in inferential thinking and explore layers of meaning and multiple perspectives and interpretations?

4. Does this book have the potential to help children learn about literary genres and narrative components and study the craft of authors and artists?

5. Does this book have the potential to help children gain insights about themselves and discover significant truths about the human experience?

6. Will this book help to expose children to the diversity in our pluralistic society? Will this book expand children's knowledge, appreciation, and understanding of those who are different from themselves? Will children see their own lives reflected in this story? Are characters who reflect children's experiences and heritage portrayed in a positive light? Is the story culturally and historically authentic?

7. Will this book generate critical reading and discussion? Will it inspire children to respond to victims of injustice with compassion? Will it challenge children to take action against injustice in their own worlds?

8. Will this book invite children to use intertextual links to generate meaning?

9. Will this book meet the learning needs and interests of individual children in the classroom? Will the collection of books selected for the classroom meet the diverse needs of all the children?

Children's Books Cited

Ada, Alma Flor. (1993). *My Name Is María Isabel*. Illustrated by K. Dyble Thompson. Translated by Ana M. Cerro. New York: Atheneum.

Aylesworth, Jim. (1999). *The Full Belly Bowl*. Illustrated by Wendy Anderson Halperin. New York: Atheneum.

Bridges, Ruby. (1999). *Through My Eyes*. Illustrated by Margo Lundell. New York: Scholastic.

Coles, Robert. (1995). *The Story of Ruby Bridges*. Illustrated by George Ford. New York: Scholastic.

Cretzmeyer, Stacy. (1994). *Your Name Is Renée: Ruth's Story as a Hidden Child: The Wartime Experiences of Ruth Kapp Hartz*. Brunswick, ME: Biddle. [Nonfiction.]

Drucker, Malka, & Halperin, Michael. (1993). *Jacob's Rescue: A Holocaust Story*. New York: Bantam.

Ezra, Mark. (1996). *The Hungry Otter*. Illustrated by Gavin Rowe. New York: Crocodile Books.

Filipovic, Zlata. (1994). *Zlata's Diary: A Child's Life in Sarajevo*. New York: Viking. [Nonfiction.]

Franklin, Kristine. (1996). *The Wolfhound*. Illustrated by Kris Waldherr. New York: Lothrop, Lee & Shepard.

Geringer, Laura, adapter. (1994). *The Seven Ravens*. Illustrated by Edward S. Gazsi. New York: HarperCollins.

Gordon, Sheila. (1987). *Waiting for the Rain*. New York: Orchard.

Gregorowski, Christopher, reteller. (2000). *Fly, Eagle, Fly! An African Tale*. Foreword by Archbishop Desmond Tutu. Illustrated by Niki Daly. New York: Margaret K. McElderry Books.

Heide, Florence Parry, & Gilliland, Judith Heide. (1992). *Sami and the Time of the Troubles*. Illustrated by Ted Lewin. New York: Clarion.

Herman, Gail. (1998). *The Lion and the Mouse*. Illustrated by Lisa McCue. New York: Random House. [Beginning reader.]

Hogrogian, Nonny, reteller and illustrator. (1985). *The Glass Mountain*. New York: Knopf.

Howard, Elizabeth Fitzgerald. (2000). *Virgie Goes to School with Us Boys*. Illustrated by E. B. Lewis. New York: Simon & Schuster.

Innocenti, Roberto, & Gallaz, Christophe. (1985). *Rose Blanche.* Translated by Martha Coventry & Richard Graglia. Mankato, MN: Creative Education.

Jiménez, Francisco. (1998). *La Mariposa.* Boston: Houghton Mifflin.

Jones, Carol. (1997). *The Lion and the Mouse.* Boston: Houghton Mifflin.

Kimmel, Eric, adapter. (1997). *Sirko and the Wolf: A Ukrainian Tale.* Illustrated by Rob Sauber. New York: Holiday House.

Kurtz, Jane. (1998). *The Storyteller's Beads.* San Diego: Harcourt Brace.

Levitin, Sonia. (1987). *The Return.* New York: Atheneum.

Matas, Carol. (1998). *Greater than Angels.* New York: Simon & Schuster.

Mochizuki, Ken. (1997). *Passage to Freedom: The Sugihara Story.* Illustrated by Dom Lee. New York: Lee & Low.

Mohr, Nicholasa. (1995). *The Magic Shell.* Illustrated by Rudy Gutierrez. New York: Scholastic.

Myers, Christopher A. (2000). *Wings.* New York: Scholastic Press.

Naidoo, Beverley. (1986). *Journey to Jo'burg: A South African Story.* New York: Lippincott.

Naylor, Phyllis Reynolds. (1991). *Shiloh.* New York: Atheneum.

Nones, Eric Jon, translator and illustrator. (1991). *The Canary Prince.* New York: Farrar, Straus, and Giroux.

Oppenheim, Joanne, adapter. (1992). *One Gift Deserves Another.* Illustrated by Bo Zaunders. New York: Dutton.

Oppenheim, Shulamith Levey. (1992). *The Lily Cupboard.* Illustrated by Ronald Himler. New York: HarperCollins.

Orgel, Doris. (2000). *The Lion and the Mouse and Other Aesop's Fables.* Illustrated by Bert Kitchen. New York: Dorling Kindersley.

Park, Frances, & Park, Ginger. (2000). *The Royal Bee.* Illustrated by Christopher Zhong-Yuan Zhang. Honesdale, PA: Boyds Mills Press.

Peet, Bill. (1972). *The Ant and the Elephant.* Boston: Houghton Mifflin.

Polacco, Patricia. (2000). *The Butterfly.* New York: Philomel Books.

Sachar, Louis. (1998). *Holes.* New York: Farrar, Straus and Giroux.

Scieszka, Jon. (1989). *The True Story of the Three Little Pigs by A. Wolf.* Illustrated by Lane Smith. New York: Viking Kestrel.

Sierra, Judy. (1997). *The Mean Hyena: A Folktale from Malawi.* Illustrated by Michael Bryant. Lodestar Books.

Snyder, Zilpha Keatley. (1985). *The Changing Maze.* Illustrated by Charles Mikolaycak. New York: Macmillan.

Spinelli, Jerry. (1990). *Maniac Magee.* New York: HarperTrophy.

Stanley, Diane. (1997). *Rumpelstiltskin's Daughter.* New York: Morrow.

Staples, Suzanne Fisher. (1989). *Shabanu: Daughter of the Wind.* New York: Knopf.

Temple, Frances. (1992). *Taste of Salt: A Story of Modern Haiti.* New York: Orchard.

Thomas, Jane Resh. (1987). *Fox in a Trap.* Illustrated by Troy Howell. New York: Clarion Books.

Tolan, Stephanie S. (1992). *Sophie and the Sidewalk Man.* Illustrated by Susan Avishai. New York: Four Winds Press.

Torre, Betty. (1990). *The Luminous Pearl: A Chinese Folktale.* Illustrated by Carol Inouye. New York: Orchard Books.

Turkle, Brinton. (1976). *Deep in the Forest.* New York: Dutton.

Watts, Bernadette, reteller. (2000). *The Lion and the Mouse: An Aesop Fable.* New York: North-South Books.

Williams, Laura E. (1996). *Behind the Bedroom Wall.* Illustrated by Nancy A. Goldstein. Minneapolis: Milkweed.

Woodson, Jacqueline. (2000). *The Other Side.* Illustrated by Earl B. Lewis. New York: Putnam's.

Yolen, Jane. (1980). "The Hundredth Dove." In Jane Yolen, *The Hundredth Dove and Other Tales.* Illustrated by David Palladini. New York: Schocken Books.

Young, Ed, reteller and illustrator. (1979). *The Lion and the Mouse: An Aesop Fable.* Garden City, NY: Doubleday.

5 The Art of Questioning

Reader Response and Literary Discussion

The view of literary discussion that informs this book emphasizes the value of readers' personal responses to literary texts. Students are invited to talk about these responses and to engage in collaborative construction of meaning in the social context of the classroom. Talking about shared texts allows students to articulate their own unique, personal, and emotional transactions with the text, along with their opinions and interpretations. In a literary discussion, students not only share and defend their own ideas, they also discover and reflect on the perspectives and interpretations of others. This type of interchange often leads students to rethink, expand, and enrich their initial transactions with texts as individual readers.

Literary discussion as defined in this book reflects the dual nature of reader response. That is, on the one hand, reading literature is an *aesthetic* experience in which readers enter into a story and participate in it as a personal and emotional experience. In the words of Louise Rosenblatt, the "aesthetic reading of a text is a unique creation, woven out of the inner life and thought of the reader" (1982, p. 277). Aesthetic readers who enter into the lives of literary characters, walk in their shoes, and see the world through their eyes have an opportunity to explore worlds beyond the boundaries of their own experience. They are able to gain new insights about what it means to be human, about the universality of human experiences as well as the uniqueness of each human being. Reading literature is also a *learning* experience when readers *step back from the text* to reflect on their own responses and interpretations, explore layers of meaning, and study the craft of the storyteller, writer, and/or artist. In most transactions with literature, readers move back and forth between affective and cognitive response, between participating in the story and stepping back to engage in inquiry, analysis, and discovery. Meaning making is learned. Teachers can support this learning by

1. demonstrating meaning-making strategies,

Segments of Chapter 5 were originally published in *Teaching Literature in the Elementary School: A Thematic Approach* by Joy F. Moss (Norwood, MA: Christopher-Gordon, 1996).

2. helping students build the literary and linguistic knowledge necessary for developing these strategies, and

3. guiding students in an exploration of the text as a resource for information, ideas, and inquiry about human experience, about the world, and about literature and the craft of writers and artists.

One of the meaning-making strategies used by readers is questioning. According to Frank Smith, comprehension of a text is related to what the reader knows and what he or she *wants to know*; comprehension means asking questions and getting answers (1988, p. 154). Reader-initiated questions shape the reading experience. The teacher can use questions as valuable teaching tools to promote aesthetic response, guide the meaning-making process, and foster higher-level thinking. At the same time, the teacher demonstrates questioning as a meaning-making strategy that students can learn to use in their independent transactions with texts. The ultimate goal is for students to generate their own questions to guide the meaning-making process and to use as learning tools that enable them to become more deeply involved in literary experiences as readers and writers. The primary goal of using teacher-initiated questions, then, is to help students discover and use the art of questioning as a basic strategy for independent reading, writing, inquiry, and learning. Teacher-initiated questions are also introduced to enrich reader response and to help students become critical readers who explore social issues in the texts they read and who ask questions about the assumptions and perspectives of the authors and illustrators of these texts.

Questions as Teaching Tools

Open-ended questions can be introduced as an integral part of shared reading experiences to invite students to talk about their personal and emotional responses to the text and to articulate their own perspectives, interpretations, and opinions. Other types of questions invite students to step back from the text in order to:

1. engage in literary analysis,

2. explore the craft and perspectives of authors and artists,

3. search for connections between diverse literary texts and between literature and life,

4. consider the perspectives and interpretations of others, and

5. probe multiple layers of meaning.

Although teacher-initiated questions encourage students to explore multiple meanings and interpretations as well as connections with literary and life experiences that take them *beyond* the text, these questions always take them *back to* the text as well. That is, the text defines the validity of responses, and students are expected to provide textual support for their interpretations, inferences, opinions, and comparative analysis.

The central purpose of this chapter is to describe various categories of questions teachers can use as teaching tools to enrich the quality of students' transactions with and responses to literary texts, and to demonstrate the art of questioning as a meaning-making strategy. Sample questions will be included for each category.

Questions Introduced *Prior* to Reading a Literary Text

In the context of a shared reading experience, the teacher sets the stage for the literary transaction by inviting the children to make predictions about the story and genre and to pose their own questions about the story. The children begin a "cover-to-cover" study of the book by examining the front and back covers, dust jacket, endpapers, dedication and title pages, author's notes, and/or other text or pictures that precede or follow the story text per se. Their predictions and questions are triggered by the title, the illustrations, what they know about the author, reteller, or illustrator, and other clues found in the "peritext" (i.e., the peripheral features that surround or enclose the verbal narrative). The quality of students' transactions with literary texts is determined in large part by the nature of the *knowledge* they bring to the text and how this knowledge is used as the story unfolds. Thus, before reading aloud, the teacher introduces questions that evoke retrieval of relevant background information for use in making predictions and comments about the story. This *prereading* discussion shows children how they can use their own background knowledge and literary histories to begin the meaning-making process even before the story begins. The sample questions below suggest the nature of prereading questions:

What does the title tell you about the story? What does the picture on the front cover tell you about the story? (Or: What do you notice on the front cover?) Children often find clues about the genre, setting, characters, and plot in the words and pictures on the front cover. Unfamiliar words in the title may need clarification. The title itself may prompt questions. For example, when *The Amiable Giant* (Slobodkin, 1955) was introduced to a group of first graders in the context of a "Giant Unit," several children asked for the meaning of the word "amiable."

The teacher suggested that they search for clues in the story to try to figure out its meaning. This search began with an examination of the title and cover illustration:

> "It probably means what *kind* of giant it is."
>
> "He *looks* like he's going to knock down those houses. 'Amiable' probably means he's a bad giant."
>
> "No. . . . I think he looks sort of sad. Maybe it means he's lonely. . . . The lonely giant."
>
> "Maybe he *is* a good giant. . . . Usually only the *good* giants get to be in the title . . . like Fin M'Coul and Glooskap." [See the children's books by Byrd (1999) and DePaola (1981) for stories about M'Coul (or MacCoul); see Norman (1989) and Bruchac (1995) for tales about Glooskap (or Gluskabe).]

As the children listened to this story about a lonely giant who looks for and finds friends, they were able to confirm, refine, or revise their initial, tentative definitions of this unfamiliar word. In this excerpt, the children were "thinking out loud" as they articulated what they noticed and what visual clues and intertextual links they used to make sense of an unfamiliar word. As the story unfolded, they continued to think out loud and to monitor their understanding as new information emerged, and they discovered that he was a "friendly giant." Later, they consulted a dictionary to confirm the meaning they had figured out from the context.

What is meant by the words "retold by" written on the front cover? This question can lead to a discussion of the nature of traditional literature, the difference between a reteller and an author, and the distinguishing characteristics of the particular genre, such as legend, fable, or folktale.

What is the copyright date? Why is this important? For example, sixth-grade students who read two novels about the Revolutionary War, *Johnny Tremain* by Esther Forbes (1943) and *My Brother Sam Is Dead* by James and Christopher Collier (1974), discovered two very different attitudes about war: the 1943 text, shaped by the World War II experience, offers a patriotic viewpoint; the 1974 text, shaped by the Vietnam War experience, offers an antiwar message. Stories about the past often reveal as much about the era in which the book was written as about the period that is recreated.

Look at the endpapers or the pages that precede the publication data page. What clues do they offer about the story? Sometimes the endpapers can best be understood *after* reading or listening to the story. For example, in *Crow Boy* by Taro Yashima (1955), the endpapers show a butterfly and a flower, respectively. After listening to this story of a boy who blossoms from a small, frightened child to a confident youth, third graders interpreted these pictures as symbols of this metamorphosis and as a reflection of a central theme of the story.

What do you think the author meant by his/her dedication? In some books the dedication can also be best understood *after* reading or listening to the story. The dedication for *Crow Boy* concludes with the words: "and to Takeo Isonaga who appears in this story as a teacher named Isobe." After listening to the story, the children returned to this dedication:

> "I think he [the author] wrote this story about *himself!* Mr. Isobe was really important for Crow Boy, and he [the author] must be Crow Boy!"
>
> "And Crow Boy liked to draw, and the author also did the pictures for this book!"
>
> "Maybe the author wrote the book to say thank you to his favorite teacher! It's sort of like *Thank You, Mr. Falker* [Patricia Polacco, 1998]. It's about a girl and the teacher who helps her learn how to read in fifth grade! She [the author] said it's her own story."

Compare the cover on the first hardcover edition of the book with later paperback editions of the book. For example, when several fifth graders examined the original hardcover edition of *Bridge to Terabithia* by Katherine Paterson (1977) along with subsequent paperback editions, they noticed that the hardcover and the 1978 paperback featured characters who could be identified as either male or female. In contrast, the 1987 paperback portrayed two characters who could easily be identified as male and female, respectively, and who appeared to be older than the characters on the covers of the earlier editions. The students attempted to explain these and other differences they found and to use this information to make predictions:

> "It's probably going to be about a *regular* friendship between a boy and girl . . . not a romantic one. See, they're younger here and in these two [the 1987 and 1998 editions] it's like the boy-girl difference isn't really important."
>
> "Even in the picture with the older kids, it doesn't look romantic. Probably the publisher put a picture of older kids on the cover to get older kids to read it. When I first saw the hardcover, they looked awful young and I didn't think I'd like it. But this one [the 1987, Harper edition] looks more interesting."

Look for other information in the text and pictures surrounding the narrative that might help you understand the story. For example, the back flap of the hardcover edition of *The King's Fountain* by Lloyd

Alexander and Ezra Jack Keats (1971) includes a few notes about the author and artist and concludes with the following:

> Collaborating for the first time, both men feel that the theme of *The King's Fountain* expresses each of their strong convictions. In his comments about the book, Mr. Keats notes that this theme is summed up in the words of the Hebrew sage, Hillel:
>
> > If I am not for myself,
> > Who will be for me?
> > And if I am only for myself,
> > What am I?
> > And if not now,
> > When?

After listening to this story, a group of fourth graders revisited these wise words to begin their discussion of the theme of this beautiful picture book. In the process, they were discovering the importance of reading each literary text "cover to cover" in order to generate meaning.

Questions Introduced *during* the Oral Presentation of a Story

Since prediction is an important strategy used in the reading process, the teacher can demonstrate this strategy by stopping at significant points and asking, ***What do you think will happen next?*** As children internalize this question, they develop an anticipatory attitude toward print, making predictions as they read or listen to a text in order to generate meaning as the story unfolds. They learn to construct a working interpretation of the story based on the clues they gather and to revise or refine this interpretation as they find new information in and generate new meaning from the unfolding text. For example, as a group of fourth graders listened to *The Mapmaker's Daughter* by Mary-Claire Helldorfer (1991), a modern fairy tale about a young girl, Suchen, who rescues a prince from an evil queen, they predicted that she would marry the prince. However, when the prince rewards her with a horse and a red cape for her next adventure, they realized that they had made their prediction based on their prior experiences with traditional fairy tales:

> "It's so different from the old tales . . . like the only thing in life for a girl was to get married. But Suchen wants to have an interesting life!"
> "This is a *modern* fairy tale. The author doesn't use the old stereotypes about men and women."
> "And the *prince* is the one to get rescued . . . by a girl!"

The teacher may decide to insert a question to call attention to a literary technique found in an unfolding story, such as a flashback, an embedded story, or alternating viewpoints. Questions about literary techniques may be used to clarify elements of the author's craft in order to assist in the meaning-making process or to provide the language of literary analysis for students to use as they explore the tools authors use to create stories. The teacher might also interrupt the story to ask a question such as, **What did that character mean by saying, "_____"?** This question helps children develop the habit of clarifying unfamiliar words and phrases that contribute to the meaning of the text and, in the process, learn a basic reading strategy: *monitoring the meaning-making process*. For example, in *The Great Quillow* (Thurber, 1944/1994), the town council members refer to the toy maker as "The Great Quillow." The reader must use the author's clues to understand that the word *great* is used as a form of mockery in one context and to express scorn in another. By the end of the story, Quillow the toy maker has managed to save the town from a giant and has earned the respect of the townspeople. The meaning of the word *great* changes significantly as the story unfolds and new information is provided.

These questions are used sparingly, of course, so that a given story can unfold with few or no interruptions. Over time, however, the teacher can demonstrate strategies of prediction and monitoring so the children can internalize these strategies and use them on their own to make sense of texts they listen to or read independently.

Questions Introduced to Encourage Aesthetic Response and to Initiate the *Post-Reading* Discussion

In her transactional theory of reading literature, Louise Rosenblatt (1978) defines the *aesthetic reader* as one who enters into a story and "lives through" it as a unique personal and emotional experience. Students are invited to share their initial reactions to the story as a whole, or to specific characters or scenes, or to the craft of the author or artist, and to share the thoughts and feelings they had as they listened to or read the story. As they share these personal responses in a group discussion, students discover that readers respond in different ways to the same text. Discovery of multiple perspectives provides opportunities for children to enrich their own understandings. The teacher can open the discussion with: **What would you like to say about this story?** Additional questions may be used to demonstrate ways in which students can articulate and reflect on their experience as they lived through the story. For example:

- As the story unfolded, did you change your mind about specific characters? Explain.

- Did any of the characters or events remind you of people or experiences in your own life? Explain.
- How did you feel about this character's behavior? Why did you think this character behaved the way he or she did? Clues?
- What do you think it would feel like to be this character?
- What did you find that was surprising, puzzling, or disturbing about the characters or events in this story?

  > For example, the fourth graders who listened to *The Mapmaker's Daughter* expressed their surprise when they discovered that this story did not end with a royal wedding as they had predicted. They learned that the mapmaker's daughter planned to set out on more adventures instead of marrying the prince.

- Which parts of this story would you like to hear or read again or share with a friend? Explain.

  > Children often talk about the segments in literary texts that they particularly enjoyed. Sharing a favorite book with a friend often begins with the words, "Listen to this!" The purpose of this question is to invite children to identify these special segments and to try to articulate *why* they found them so interesting or compelling. In the process, they may discover something about the author's craft.

Questions Introduced to Guide Literary Analysis

After students have had opportunities to share and reflect on their personal responses to the text, they are invited to step back from the text and engage in literary analysis as an integral part of the meaning-making process. Teachers introduce questions that call attention to literary elements (e.g., setting, plot, characters, theme, style, viewpoint), genre, and author's craft, or the choices authors make as they use these elements and literary techniques to create narratives. As students identify literary elements, the relationships between them, and the role of a particular element in the story as a whole, they can begin to generate meaning through inference, interpretation, and the use of prior literary knowledge and personal experience. For example, a group of fourth graders was asked to talk about *setting* after they had listened to Katherine Paterson's *The King's Equal* (1992). An excerpt from the resulting discussion illustrates the students' collaborative meaning making as well as the potential of this modern fairy tale to stimulate interpretive exploration:

> "There're *two* settings. . . . One is the palace where the prince is, and one is the mountain shack where Rosamund lives."

"The settings are opposite. . . . One's rich and one's poor."

[Teacher: *"What technique is the author using here?"*]

"I remember. . . . It's like those two-stories-in-one we read."

"It's the 'story-in-a-story' technique!"

"But these are more like side-by-side stories. One's about the prince, and one's about Rosamund. . . ."

"It's like those parallel lines on our math chart [points to the wall chart]."

[Teacher: "Yes! There's even a literary term for this: *parallel plot.*"]

"You could *draw* this plot . . . like on the chart. You could make the lines go like this [using his hands to demonstrate] for the two stories and then they intersect when the two stories come together . . . when she came to the *palace* to meet the prince."

"That's a good idea. . . . It would look like this [shows his sketch in progress]: See, before they meet, the lines are parallel; then they intersect here at the palace; then the lines get parallel again when they switch places . . . when the prince goes to live in the *shack* to prove he can do it and Rosamund lives in the *palace!*"

"And the stories intersect *again* when the prince comes back to the palace and she agrees to marry him [shows her own sketch]."

"The author really planned this story carefully. When that greedy prince switched places, he learned what it *feels* like to be poor and hungry and not have servants! And this is when he changes."

". . . and she had to be in the palace to fix up the mess he made when he took all the money and food from the people."

"I liked the way the author did this story. . . . In the old stories the prince looked for someone who's good enough for *him*, but in this story, he has to prove *he's* good enough for *her!*"

"I think that's the theme! When they switched places, he learned what's *really* important . . . that money isn't everything . . . ."

"I get it now! He learned that someone with friends is *richer* than someone with gold . . . and that's why Rosamund finally said she'd marry him!"

"Also, I think she wanted to see if he could learn to do things for himself."

"And he learned how to be *kind*. He really changed a lot!"

[Teacher: "A character who changes during the story is called a *dynamic character.*"]

"Maybe the author wanted you to think about stereotypes about men *and* women. Rosamund was gentle and caring *and* intelligent and independent, and the prince had to *learn* how to be gentle and caring! That was a switch, too!"

The teacher's questions about this story's setting and about the technique the author used to develop the setting helped the children retrieve their knowledge of the literary technique they had studied earlier, the story-within-a-story. This enabled them to move on to the thoughtful discussion of the author's craft recorded above. In the course of the children's collaborative analysis of this story, the teacher introduced terms used for several literary concepts the children articulated as they explored character, plot, and theme.

Rebecca Lukens's *A Critical Handbook of Children's Literature* (1999) is a very useful resource for teachers who want to review literary elements, techniques, and genres in order to formulate questions that guide children's analysis of narrative and introduce the language of literary analysis to enrich their study of literature.

Questions That Help Students Appreciate the Craft of Authors and Artists

The students who responded to *The King's Equal* revealed their appreciation of the author's craft. They figured out some of the choices Katherine Paterson had made to create this story, as well as the relationship between the setting and the development of characters, plot, and theme. Teachers can introduce questions designed to call attention to author's craft by focusing on literary techniques such as story-within-a story and on the use of viewpoint, traditional forms and motifs, and literary genres. For example:

Whose story is it? Why do you think the author chose this character's version of events? One way authors shape a story is through the use of viewpoint, the perspective from which the story is told. In *The True Story of the Three Little Pigs by A. Wolf* (Scieszka, 1989), a modern illustrated revision of the traditional tale, Alexander T. Wolf tells his *own* version of what happened when he encountered the three pigs. *A Frog Prince* by Alix Berenzy (1989), another modern *viewpoint revision* of a traditional tale, is told from the frog's point of view because the author's sympathies were with the frog instead of the spoiled princess in the Grimm tale. *Cinderella's Rat* (Meddaugh, 1997), another picture book, is told from the viewpoint of the rat who was transformed into a coachman by Cinderella's fairy godmother. *I Was a Rat!* (Pullman, 2000) is a novel told from the perspective of Cinderella's rat-turned-pageboy.

The critical study of a historical novel or memoir begins with the identification of the perspective from which the story is told. *No Pretty Pictures: A Child of War* by Anita Lobel (1998) is a first-person account of the author's childhood after the Nazis came to her comfortable home in Krakow, Poland. *Four Perfect Pebbles: A Holocaust Story* (Perl and Lazan, 1996) is Marion Blumenthal Lazan's memoir of her childhood, the six and a half years she and her parents and brother lived in refugee, transit, and prison camps. *Behind the Bedroom Wall* (Williams, 1996) is a story told from the perspective of a thirteen-year-old girl who is an ardent member of the local Nazi youth group in Germany. *Parallel Journeys* (Ayer, Waterford, & Heck, 1995) juxtaposes excerpts from two autobiographies of individuals who lived through World War II and whose stories are told in alternating chapters. One perspective is offered by Alfons, who attained a high rank in the Hitler Youth; another perspective is offered by Helen, a Jewish girl who ended up in Auschwitz.

Examples of questions about the craft of artists are listed below:

- How did the artist show the feelings of the characters?
- How did the artist's choice of media help to express the mood of the story?
- How would this story be different without the illustrations?
- Compare/contrast two or more artists' interpretations of a traditional fairy tale. What choices did they make?

> For example, a group of third graders compared several illustrated retellings of the traditional Beauty and the Beast tale. They were especially intrigued with Jan Brett's illustrated retelling of this French fairy tale (1989). As the story unfolded in the read-aloud session, the children noticed that the engravings on the stone wall in the Beast's garden and the tapestries in his palace reveal humans engaged in the same actions as the animals that serve Beauty or play music for her. The children discussed the possibility that Brett created these parallels between the story characters and the tapestries to show life in the palace *before* the prince and his servants were transformed into animals prior to the beginning of the story. After listening to the whole story and paying close attention to the illustrations, the children discovered that the written messages woven into the tapestries had foreshadowed the plot and theme development. They wanted to hear the story again and to search for details they had missed during the first reading. One child commented: "Now we'll be able to read the pictures better. She [Brett] decided to use the pictures to tell some of the story that's not in the words!"

Questions That Encourage Students to Search for and Use *Intertextual Links* to Generate Meaning

Teachers can introduce questions that encourage students to

1. draw from their literary histories, personal experiences, and

knowledge to generate meaning in their transactions with literary texts, and

2. build a "literary data bank" about genres, character types, motifs, patterns, themes, narrative elements, literary devices, and literary language.

Students learn to approach each new text in light of previous literary experiences and their store of literary knowledge and to identify *intertextual links* to generate meaning. For example, the discussion of Katherine Paterson's *The King's Equal* was enriched by the students' previous experiences with embedded stories or parallel-plot patterns. Their recognition of this literary technique enabled the students to focus on the way the author used this structure to develop the two central characters. As they listened to the story, these students were sitting at their desks, which were arranged in a circle, and they had been invited to draw or write something of interest about the story as it unfolded. Sketching a diagram of the parallel plot seemed to help many of the children visualize this plot structure in order to comprehend the story as a whole. These students also identified the intertextual link between this story and traditional fairy tales featuring the search for a bride. Using this link as a springboard, these fourth graders took the next step in the meaning-making process: they identified Paterson's *revision* of this traditional pattern, which, in turn, led them to an exploration of the central theme of this modern fairy tale.

An *intertextually rich environment* can be created when the literature program is structured around cumulative experiences in which students are introduced to carefully selected, conceptually related texts in order to optimize their discovery of increasingly complex connections between diverse texts. Examples of questions used to generate *comparative analysis* of related texts and to spark the search for intertextual links are listed below:

We have been reading traditional fables from different countries. How are these stories similar? How would you define a fable? After identifying recurring patterns in these fables, a group of second graders formulated a definition of this literary genre. The next step for these students was to test the validity of their definition. To this end, the children listened to several additional fables and analyzed each one in terms of the distinguishing characteristics included in their definition. After relevant revisions were made and a consensus reached, their final definition was used as a starting point for a writing project in which the children created their own fables.

Compare Leo Lionni's modern fables with the traditional fables of Aesop. What similarities and differences do you find? What can you say about the differences between Aesop and Lionni in terms of their assumptions and beliefs about the human experience? These questions were introduced to fourth and fifth graders who were engaged in an in-depth study of traditional and modern fables. For example, they compared Lionni's *Frederick* (1967) with Aesop's "The Ant and the Grasshopper." Frederick the mouse did not collect grain with the other mice in preparation for the long winter, but these hardworking mice accepted Frederick's uniqueness. His poetry provided food for the mind, the spirit, and imagination during the dark days of winter. Lionni's modern fable reflects his belief in the importance of individual differences, the value of the arts in our lives, and the adage that human beings do not live "by bread alone." *Frederick* presents a sharp contrast with the harsh justice and work ethic pronounced by Aesop's ants, who turned their backs on the starving grasshopper when he begged for food. They said, "All summer long you made nothing but music. Now all winter long you can dance!"(Pinkney, 2000, p. 12). A survey of a number of collections of Aesop's fables revealed that most retellings of "The Ant and the Grasshopper" end with this harsh statement. However, a recent illustrated retelling by Amy Lowry Poole (2000) invites a new look at this old fable. Poole's *The Ant and the Grasshopper* is set in the Imperial Chinese Emperor's Summer Palace. The grasshopper danced and sang for the royal family while the industrious ants gathered grain for the winter, warning the grasshopper to prepare for the cold and snow. When winter arrived, the Emperor and his court left the Summer Palace and the ants "closed their door against the ice and snow" (unpaged). The story ends with the words: "And the grasshopper huddled beneath the palace eaves and rubbed his hands together in a mournful chirp, wishing he had heeded the ant's advice" (unpaged). The pictures, however, tell another story. Throughout the story, the artist depicts a young boy who watches the ants at work. The boy collects food in a basket and leaves it for the grasshopper before he departs from the Summer Palace. A small group of students examined this unique version and identified clues in the text and pictures to infer Poole's assumptions about human nature.

The main characters in these stories have similar problems. How does each character attempt to solve his or her problem? What are important differences in their responses or decisions? These questions were introduced to fifth-grade students who were focusing on the inner conflicts of characters in contemporary realistic fiction.

How do the characters in this group of stories respond to injustice? This question invited students to engage in a critical, in-depth study of stories that address social issues associated with differences in race, religion, gender, class, and ability. For example, *The Other Side* (Woodson, 2001) is a picture book that opens with the words: "That summer the fence that stretched through our town seemed bigger" (unpaged). The fence separates the Black side of town from the White side. Clover, an African American girl who lives on one side of the fence, watches the White girl, Annie, who lives on the other side. Both girls have been told to stay on their own side. Eventually, the girls find a way around this racial barrier constructed and maintained by adults on both sides. In her own words, Clover tells the story of the summer she and Annie become friends. On the last page of the book, Annie comments: "Someday somebody's going to come along and knock this old fence down." Clover nods and says: "Yeah. . . . Someday" (unpaged). This poignant story invites readers and listeners to talk about the injustice felt by both girls and their response to the racial division in this rural community. This picture book was read aloud to older students to introduce a unit of study addressing a provocative subject and to demonstrate ways to respond as critical readers to literary texts that address complex social issues. In her book *Teaching with Picture Books in the Middle School*, Iris Tiedt introduces middle-grade teachers to the "wonderful possibilities of the picture book" and highlights the value of the picture book as a stimulus for classroom discussion (Tiedt, 2000, p. 2).

Maniac Magee (Spinelli, 1990) is a novel about another racially divided town, Two Mills, Pennsylvania, in which the East End and West End are two hostile camps separated by Hector Street. Maniac Magee, a legendary hero in a contemporary realistic novel, crosses Hector Street and moves between these hostile camps in an attempt to break down barriers and build bridges between those who are different. This larger-than-life character confronts the prejudice, ignorance, and fear that he finds on both sides of Hector Street, fear of the same type that Clover finds on both sides of the fence in *The Other Side*. Unlike the unstated context in Woodson's story, the racial tensions that serve as the context in Spinelli's story are clearly defined.

The Storyteller's Beads (Kurtz, 1998), an example of historical realism, is set during the famine and political strife in Ethiopia in the 1980s. It is the story of Sahay, a Christian girl, and Rahel, a blind Jewish girl, who escape their native Ethiopia and set out on the dangerous journey across the desert and, eventually, to Jerusalem. These two girls, who had been taught to hate and fear the other, manage to overcome cultural prejudices, become friends, and help each other survive. As in the other stories selected for this study of social issues associated with diversity, the central characters in *The Storyteller's Beads* take action against injustice and break down social barriers.

   Identify examples of journey tales in this group of stories. What are the different meanings of the word* journey? *Talk about the different kinds of journeys you found in these stories. For example, *Journey* (MacLachlan, 1991) is about a boy's search for the truth about his past and about his mother, who has abandoned him and his sister. The title of this novel refers not only to an inward journey but also to the name of the protagonist and to the physical journey taken by his mother in response to an inner restlessness. Fourth graders who read this book explored the differences between emotional and physical journeys. They discovered that the protagonist's search for truth guided his emotional journey. His quest ends successfully when he is able to confront the truth and to accept the cold reality of abandonment so that he can move on with his life.

   A study of the *quest pattern* can also be the focus of thematic units featuring traditional literature and modern fantasy. The *quest or journey tale* is an almost universal story pattern, according to Joseph Campbell, who describes in *The Hero with a Thousand Faces* (1949/1968) the initiation journey of departure, adventure, trials, tests, and return. Whether the story is about Peter Rabbit's quest for adventure, Max's quest for inner control in *Where the Wild Things Are* (Sendak, 1963), Theseus's journey to Crete to slay the Minotaur, Leje's quest for his mother's stolen brocade in *The Weaving of a Dream* (Heyer, 1986), or the young girl who seeks her beloved in the castle that lies east of the sun and west of the moon in a translated Norwegian fairy tale (Dasent, 1991), the heroes and heroines leave home, set out on a journey, survive a series of tests and ordeals, and return home triumphant.

Questions That Invite Students to Explore Connections between Literature and Life

Teachers introduce questions to build bridges between the story world and the child's own world of reality, imagination, and dreams. Children are invited to consider the story in light of their own experiences and values and to identify with a character's feelings and concerns. They are given opportunities to gain insights about their own lives and to expand their thinking beyond *what is* to *what could be*. Students are also asked to step back from the text and to respond to it objectively, using information from relevant outside sources whenever appropriate. Questions are introduced to invite subjective as well as objective evaluation of the story.

A few examples of questions introduced to elicit *subjective evaluation* based on children's personal experiences and their inner lives are included below:

- Do you think this story could really happen? Explain.
- How did you feel about this character? Did you change your mind about this character as you listened to the story? Explain.
- Has this ever happened to you? Did you ever feel this way? Explain.
- Who do you know who is like this character? How are they similar?
- What do you think this character will do the *next* time something like this happens?

Examples of questions introduced to stimulate *imaginative thinking and dreaming* in response to the story:

- What would *you* have done with those three wishes?
- This character really wanted to become an artist. What do *you* really want to become?
- What if *you* found a baby dragon that had been left alone when its mother was killed? (This is the challenge faced by Derek in *The Dragonling* by Jackie French Koller [1990].)

Examples of questions designed to elicit *objective evaluation*:

- What did you think about the way the problem was solved in this story?
- Did you think the ending was realistic? Explain.
- What did the author do to make the characters and events believable?
- Do you think the author had strong feelings about a particular issue? Explain.
- Can you identify any story characters who protested against injustice and inequities and/or provided insight and wisdom? Explain.
- Look at the copyright date for this story. What is the relationship between the content or theme of the story and the social-political context of the author? (For example, Eve Bunting's *Fly Away Home* (1991), Stephanie Tolan's *Sophie and the Sidewalk Man* (1992), and Paula Fox's novel *Monkey Island* (1991) all feature homelessness, a significant social problem that received increasing public awareness and attention in the 1990s.)
- Do you think the author revealed his or her *own* attitudes? biases? opinions? Explain.

- How would you determine whether the events in this histori-cal novel are accurately described? (An Author's Note or refer-ence texts in the library could be consulted.)
- Would you recommend this book to a friend? Why or why not?

The Art of Teaching, the Art of Questioning, and a Note of Caution

The art of teaching is, in large part, the art of asking significant, well-timed questions that stretch students' minds and imaginations and that help them move toward growth and understanding as independent learners. Questioning is a *teaching tool* that can be used to help students discover the art of questioning as a *learning tool* and as a reading strat-egy. The types of questions featured in this chapter were designed to enrich children's literary experiences and to foster thoughtful and per-sonally meaningful responses to literature. Questions can be used to guide the meaning-making process throughout group read-aloud ses-sions: (1) prior to the oral reading of the literary text, (2) as the students enter into and respond to the unfolding text, and (3) after the oral read-ing. Initial predictions are confirmed, refined, or revised, and initial un-derstandings are expanded and/or modified as students gain new in-formation from the unfolding text. During the post-reading discussion, students share their personal responses, understandings, and interpre-tations and consider other students' perspectives and conclusions that differ from their own. In the context of ongoing, cumulative literary discussions, readers form an interpretive community in which they negotiate group-constructed meanings. In the process, *teacher-initiated questions are gradually replaced by questions initiated by students* who are ready to direct their own literary explorations and learning experiences.

A note of *caution,* however, is in order at this point. The sample questions included in this chapter are offered as *general suggestions* and should be used sparingly. Too many questions can turn the enjoyment of literary exploration and discovery into the drudgery of meaningless drill. Furthermore, the sample questions included here were originally formulated to challenge specific groups of children from kindergarten through grade 6. In order to formulate questions for their *own* students, teachers need to consider the age, experience, and learning needs of their students as well as these students' level of involvement and interest in a particular literary text at a given time. The children who entered into each of the group discussions featured in this book were quite diverse in terms of language and cognitive ability, experiential background, learning styles, needs, attitudes, and social/emotional development.

The teacher's challenge was to enable *all* the children to become active participants in each of these group discussions of shared literary texts. Most of the questions introduced in these read-aloud sessions were open-ended in order to encourage diverse responses and to help children think in terms of possibilities and multiple meanings and perspectives rather than looking for a single, "correct" answer. The questions introduced in each group session varied in their level of difficulty so that every child could be appropriately challenged at his or her ability level. However, read-aloud sessions often "leveled the playing field" for many of the children who were less proficient or experienced as readers than were their peers. Many of these children enjoyed great success as thoughtful and insightful contributors to the collaborative process of literary study in these group sessions. They were able to respond to increasingly complex literary texts and engage in the meaning-making process unlimited by their skills as readers. At the same time, they were given opportunities to learn about literature and about the craft of authors and artists and to practice strategies that proficient readers use to read literature.

Different types of questions were presented in this chapter to suggest some of the *possibilities* for creating rich literary experiences in which students engage in lively discussion as they explore multiple layers of meaning and the craft of authors and artists. The ultimate goal is for students to initiate their own questions to generate meaning as readers and writers and to give themselves a springboard for inquiry and discovery, thinking and learning, as they respond to shared literary texts in the social context of the classroom.

Children's Books Cited

Alexander, Lloyd. (1971). *The King's Fountain.* Illustrated by Ezra Jack Keats. New York: E. P. Dutton.

Ayer, Eleanor H., with Waterford, Helen, & Heck, Alfons. (1995). *Parallel Journeys.* New York: Atheneum.

Berenzy, Alix. (1989). *A Frog Prince.* New York: Henry Holt.

Brett, Jan, reteller and illustrator. (1989). *Beauty and the Beast.* New York: Clarion.

Bruchac, Joseph, reteller. (1995). *Gluskabe and the Four Wishes.* Illustrated by Christine Nyburg Shrader. New York: Cobblehill/Dutton. [An Abenaki tale.]

Bunting, Eve. (1991). *Fly Away Home.* Illustrated by Ronald Himler. New York: Clarion.

Byrd, Robert. (1999). *Finn MacCoul and His Fearless Wife: A Giant of a Tale from Ireland*. New York: Dutton Children's Books.

Collier, James, & Collier, Christopher. (1974). *My Brother Sam Is Dead*. New York: Four Winds.

Dasent, George Webbe, translator. (1991). *East o' the Sun and West o' the Moon*. Illustrated by Patrick James Lynch. Cambridge, MA: Candlewick Press. [A Norwegian fairy tale.]

DePaola, Tomie, reteller. (1981). *Fin M'Coul: The Giant of Knockmany Hill*. New York: Holiday House. [An Irish tale.]

Forbes, Esther. (1943). *Johnny Tremain: A Novel for Young & Old*. Illustrated by Lynd Ward. Boston: Houghton Mifflin.

Fox, Paula. (1991). *Monkey Island*. New York: Orchard Books.

Helldorfer, Mary-Claire. (1991). *The Mapmaker's Daughter*. Illustrated by Jonathan Hunt. New York: Bradbury Press.

Heyer, Marilee, reteller. (1986). *The Weaving of a Dream: A Chinese Folktale*. New York: Viking.

Koller, Jackie French. (1990). *The Dragonling*. Illustrated by Judith Mitchell. Boston: Little, Brown.

Kurtz, Jane. (1998). *The Storyteller's Beads*. New York: Harcourt Brace.

Lionni, Leo. (1967). *Frederick*. New York: Pantheon.

Lobel, Anita. (1998). *No Pretty Pictures: A Child of War*. New York: Greenwillow.

MacLachlan, Patricia. (1991). *Journey*. New York: Delacorte.

Meddaugh, Susan. (1997). *Cinderella's Rat*. Boston: Houghton Mifflin.

Norman, Howard A., reteller. (1989). *How Glooskap Outwits the Ice Giants and Other Tales of the Maritime Indians*. Wood Engravings by Michael McCurdy. Boston: Little, Brown.

Paterson, Katherine. (1977). *Bridge to Terabithia*. Illustrated by Donna Diamond. New York: Crowell.

Paterson, Katherine. (1992). *The King's Equal*. Illustrated by Vladimir Vasil'evich Vagin. New York: HarperCollins.

Paxton, reteller. (1996). *The Ant and the Grasshopper: An Aesop's Fable*. Illustrated by Philip Webb. Glenview, IL: Celebration Press.

Perl, Lila, & Lazan, Marion Blumenthal. (1996). *Four Perfect Pebbles: A Holocaust Story*. New York: Greenwillow.

Pinkney, Jerry, illustrator. (2000). "The Grasshopper and the Ants." In *Aesop's Fables* (pp. 12–13). New York: SeaStar Books.

Polacco, Patricia. (1998). *Thank You, Mr. Falker*. New York: Philomel.

Poole, Amy Lowry, reteller and illustrator. (2000). *The Ant and the Grasshopper*. New York: Holiday House.

Pullman, Philip. (2000). *I Was a Rat!* Illustrated by Kevin Hawkes. New York: Knopf.

Scieszka, Jon. (1989*).The True Story of the Three Little Pigs by A. Wolf.* Illustrated by Lane Smith. New York: Viking Kestrel.

Sendak, Maurice. (1963). *Where the Wild Things Are.* New York: Harper & Row.

Slobodkin, Louis. (1955). *The Amiable Giant.* New York: Vanguard Press.

Spinelli, Jerry. (1990). *Maniac Magee.* New York: HarperTrophy.

Thurber, James. (1944/1994).*The Great Quillow.* Illustrated by Steven Kellogg. San Diego: Harcourt Brace.

Tolan, Stephanie S. (1992). *Sophie and the Sidewalk Man.* Illustrated by Susan Avishai. New York: Four Winds Press.

Williams, Laura E. (1996). *Behind the Bedroom Wall.* Illustrated by Nancy A. Goldstein. Minneapolis: Milkweed.

Woodson, Jacqueline. (2001). *The Other Side.* Illustrated by Earl B. Lewis. New York: Putnam's.

Yashima, Taro. (1955). *Crow Boy.* New York: Viking.

6 Personalized Reading

Literary Discussion and Personalized Reading

Literary discussion sets the stage for personalized reading. Literary discussion, as defined in this book, evolves in response to shared texts in the social context of group literary experiences. Shared texts selected by the teacher are introduced to the whole class. Personalized reading, on the other hand, implies a solitary reader who reads self-selected texts. However, there is a synergistic relationship between literary discussion in response to shared texts and reader response in the context of personalized reading. Literary discussion can motivate students to develop the reading habit and prepare them to become thoughtful, engaged readers. Literary discussion gives students opportunities to develop literary and linguistic knowledge that will enrich the quality of their experiences as independent readers and the quality of the literature they select to read for personal pleasure and growth. In turn, solitary readers draw from their independent reading experiences to contribute to and enrich the literary discussion of shared texts. Solitary readers can also extend their personal reading experiences by entering into informal dialogue with other readers about self-selected texts.

Becoming Engaged Readers: Motivation

Literacy programs that teach children the knowledge and strategies they need to become proficient readers and writers should also be designed to motivate children to *want* to read and write. Using the term "aliterate" to describe "a person who knows how to read but who doesn't choose to read," Bernice Cullinan has expressed concern about the prevalence of aliteracy in our society (1987, p. 11). Subsequent research has focused on the decline in positive reading attitudes and voluntary reading as children progress through school (Anderson, Wilson, and Fielding, 1988; McKenna, Ellsworth, and Kear, 1995). Researchers have found that authentic literary experiences and opportunities to read self-selected material in school serve as powerful motivational factors in encouraging children to develop the reading habit and to become engaged and involved readers (Allington, 1994; Fink, 1995–96; Langford and Allen, 1983; and Turner, 1995). For example, Fink found that the dyslexic students he studied reached the highest level of reading competence through voluntary reading of personally interesting materials. Wigfield and Guthrie (1995) developed a questionnaire called the Motivations for Reading Questionnaire to assess the dimensions of motivation and used this instrument to determine the extent to which each of these dimensions correlate with reading frequency. They found that the strongest correlates with reading frequency were (1) intrinsic motivations such as curiosity and aesthetic enjoyment of experiencing different kinds of literary or informational texts and (2) children's sense that they can be successful as readers. In a discussion of the implications of these results, the authors of this study suggested that teachers can promote children's reading motivation by (1) fostering children's sense that they *can read*, by providing opportunities for successful experiences with reading, and (2) building student choice of reading materials into the instructional program to develop and support individual interests and curiosity.

According to these and other research findings, teachers who incorporate student choice and voluntary reading into their literacy/literary programs foster positive reading attitudes and achievement. In addition, studies show that teachers who love to read serve as models for their students. Some teachers demonstrate their love of books by reading their own choices along with their students during the time set aside for self-selected, independent reading. Other teachers read what their students have selected, discuss what they are reading, and exchange recommendations for further reading. Probably the most powerful modeling is done during the read-aloud sessions that serve as the context for literary discussion of shared texts. Students see their teacher as an enthusiastic reader and student of literature, actively involved in literary transactions. At the same time, as these students share personal responses, interpretations, and insights during ongoing literary discussions that evolve out of shared texts, they see the active involvement of their peers in transactions with literature. As students share their reading experiences and personal responses with others in a supportive environment, they become part of a *community of readers* (Hepler and Hickman, 1982). In such a community, enthusiasm about books and reading is often contagious. In the context of cumulative literary discussions of shared texts, students discover new possibilities for personal reading, new ways to think about literature, and new connections with their peers.

In a classic article in *The Reading Teacher,* Lyman C. Hunt Jr. focused on reading as a quest for meaning and warned that "Preoccupation with keeping track of and correcting errors interferes with attending to meaningful reading" (1970/1996–97, p. 279). Hunt highlighted the significance of self-selection, interest, and motivation for successful reading experiences: "Every observant teacher has seen the highly motivated reader engrossed in a book which, for him, is obviously of considerable difficulty. But because interest and involvement are high, he persists in the pursuit of ideas and he gets some" (p. 279). Hunt recommended student choice and opportunities for silent reading to allow readers to engage in a personal quest for ideas. "Uninterrupted Sustained Silent Reading is the essence of reading power; the ability to keep going with ideas in print. Without it the reader is crippled; with the power of sustained silent reading the reader is on his own, he can propel himself through print" (p. 281).

Selecting Personally Interesting Books: Exposure

Children who are exposed to the world of books and are invited to explore this rich world of language, ideas, and human experience in the form of diverse genres (i.e., poetry, fable, myth, legend, folktale, fairy tale, contemporary and historical fiction, fantasy, mystery, adventure, biography, and so on) are being prepared for knowledgeable self-selection of books for personal reading pleasure. Children differ significantly in their prior knowledge, experience, capacities, attitudes, and interests, and teachers can respond to these individual differences by promoting student choice and voluntary reading in the classroom. The teacher serves as a guide and partner in the exploration of the literary world by introducing children to diverse genres in traditional and modern literature and a wide range of topics, authors, and artists. Exposure to this literary world is a central feature of the literature program that is structured around discussion of the texts selected by the teacher for shared reading experiences. Exposing children to this literary world expands their *awareness* of what is available to them. The ultimate goal is for children to explore this world of possibilities on their own. The following examples suggest how shared texts selected by the teacher, along with the literary discussion that evolves in response to these texts, can become springboards for developing personalized reading interests.

Traditional Folktales

After listening to and discussing a variety of traditional folktales in a series of group sessions, a second-grade boy asked the teacher, "Where did you find all those good stories?" In response to this question, the teacher introduced the children to the "398 section" in the library and to the nature of the books identified as traditional literature and shelved in this section. Many of the children were delighted with this "discovery" and returned again and again to these shelves when selecting books for independent reading. As a result, they developed new reading interests as they explored the treasures in this part of the literary world! When these children shared these treasures with their friends, new explorers began their search in this rich reservoir of reading pleasure.

Thematic Unit Featuring Dogs in Fiction and Nonfiction

When the teacher held up the book *Pinkerton, Behave* by Steven Kellogg (1979) in the context of a thematic unit featuring dogs in fiction and nonfiction, several students recognized this author/artist and shared what they knew about his humorous tales. After this book was read aloud and discussed, other children requested "more Kellogg books." In response, the teacher set up a display of the books written and illustrated by Kellogg, as well as the books he had illustrated for other authors. Some of the children selected books from this display because they already knew and loved Kellogg's books. Others selected books from the Pinkerton series because they loved dogs. Others had never heard of Kellogg or his books and were delighted to discover "these funny stories." The children read these books independently or with a partner in the classroom, or they took a book home to read with a parent or older sibling.

The literary unit featuring dogs was developed with children in grades 1 and 2 in response to numerous requests for dog stories. This thematic unit was designed to provide the children with opportunities to explore diverse literary genres including legends, folktales, fantasy, realism, humor, poetry, and nonfiction and to discover new books related to a current interest or to discover a new area of interest for independent reading. The teacher selected books to read aloud in a series of group sessions and set up a display of related books from which the children could choose titles of interest for independent reading. This display included books for beginning readers as well as those with more experience and proficiency. The titles on display were selected to encourage transition readers to move into longer stories in chapter books. When *The Bravest Dog Ever: The True Story of Balto* (Standiford, 1989) was read aloud, one child commented that she was going to tell an absent classmate about this book: "She just loves sled dogs, and I know she'll like this book!" It is interesting to note that in a "community of readers" children develop an awareness of the special interests of their peers and respond accordingly. When other children expressed an interest in sled dogs and the Iditarod Race, in particular, the teacher suggested a number of related fiction and nonfiction titles for independent reading, such as *A Sled Dog for Moshi* (Bushey, 1994); *Stone Fox* (Gardiner, 1980); *Adventure in Alaska* (Kramer, 1993); *Silver* (Whelan, 1988); *Dogteam* (Paulsen, 1993); *Iditarod Dream* (Wood, 1996); *Akiak: A Tale from the Iditarod* (Blake, 1997), and *Balto and the Great Race* (Kimmel and Koerber, 1999).

Long after this particular thematic unit had been concluded, the children continued to return to specific titles, authors, genres, or topics that had been introduced during the unit. Again, they had found new possibilities for personal reading pleasure, and many were delighted to discover that they were ready to read the longer stories with more continuous text found in the chapter books displayed alongside the books for beginning and transition readers. Motivated to pursue a personal interest, these young readers were willing to try more challenging reading material and, in the process, developed a sense of their own growth as readers.

Thematic Unit on Myths

In the context of a literary thematic unit featuring myths, a group of fourth-grade students was introduced to a variety of illustrated editions of single tales, such as *Wings* (Yolen, 1991), *Theseus and the Minotaur* (Fisher, 1988), *The Trojan Horse* (Hutton, 1992), *Cyclops* (Fisher, 1991), *Pegasus* (Mayer, 1998), *Pegasus, the Flying Horse* (Yolen, 1998), *King Midas* (Stewig, 1999), *King Midas and the Golden Touch* (Craft, 1999), *Arachne Speaks* (Hovey, 2000), and *Atalanta's Race* (Climo, 1995). These single editions were read aloud and discussed in a series of cumulative, whole-group literary discussions. In addition, the teacher set up a display of illustrated collections of myths from diverse cultures, such as *Book of Greek Myths* (D'Aulaire & D'Aulaire, 1962), *The Wanderings of Odysseus: The Story of the Odyssey* (Sutcliff, 1996), *The Adventures of Odysseus* (Philip, 1997), *Apollo & Daphne: Masterpieces of Mythology* (Barber, 1998), *Greek Myths* (Morley, 1998), *Greek Gods and Goddesses* (McCaughrean, 1998), *The Book of Goddesses* (Waldherr, 1995), *Celtic Myths* (McBratney, 1998), *Favorite Norse Myths* (Osborne, 1996), *Odin's Family: Myths of the Vikings* (Philip, 1996), and *The Bronze Cauldron: Myths and Legends of the World* (McCaughrean, 1998), as well as longer texts for more advanced readers, such as *The Trojan War* (Coolidge, 1952). Students were invited to select these books for independent reading and to share intertextual links and other discoveries in the group discussions. By the end of this literary unit, many of the children added mythology to their list of special interests for personal reading.

Variants of Traditional Tales

Literary thematic units for elementary school children can be designed to include traditional and modern stories and informational books that feature cultural, social, and personal diversity. When books are selected to reflect the diversity in our society and, more specifically, in our classrooms, children are given opportunities to learn about the many ways people are different as well as the many more ways they are similar. Books can open doors to cultures and life experiences that are new to some children, and they can provide mirrors to reflect the cultures and life experiences of other children. During a thematic unit featuring variants of traditional tales, a child whose parents were from Korea was very excited to discover *The Korean Cinderella* (Climo, 1993) in the display of variants. For the first time, this child began to share with her classmates information about her own cultural heritage, starting with the pictures in this illustrated edition. In fact, she brought to school a Korean dress that was very similar to those pictured in this text. This prompted several of her classmates to look for variants that reflected their own cultural heritage. For example, children with Hispanic backgrounds discovered and shared with their classmates *Paco and the Witch* (Pitre, 1995), a Puerto Rican variant of the Rumpelstiltskin story, *The Rainbow-Colored Horse* (Belpré, 1978), a Puerto Rican variant of the Cinderella story, and *Princess Florecita and the Iron Shoes* (Stewig, 1995), a Spanish variant of Sleeping Beauty. A Chinese American boy was surprised to find four variants from China: *Yeh-Shen: A Cinderella Story from China* (Louie, 1982); *Lon Po Po: A Red-Riding Hood Story from China* (Young, 1989); *Little Plum* (Young, 1994), a Chinese variant of the Tom Thumb story; and *The Dragon Prince: A Chinese Beauty and the Beast Tale* (Yep, 1997). Several African American children found an African variant of Cinderella, *Mufaro's Beautiful Daughters* (Steptoe, 1987), as well as two Creole variants of this tale, *The Talking Eggs: A Folktale from the American South* (San Souci, 1989) and *Cendrillon: A Caribbean Cinderella* (San Souci, 1998). The children were also delighted to find other variants of the Cinderella tale, such as *The Golden Sandal: A Middle-Eastern Cinderella Story* (Hickox, 1998), *The Way Meat Loves Salt: A Cinderella Tale from the Jewish Tradition* (Jaffe, 1998), and *Angkat, the Cambodian Cinderella* (Coburn, 1998), as well as a new retelling of a Rumpelstiltskin variant: *The Girl Who Spun Gold* (Hamilton, 2000). This variant from the West Indies is beautifully illustrated by Leo and Diane Dillon. The thematic unit planned by the teacher as an introduction to variants of traditional tales proved to be a springboard for an ongoing search for reading material that reflected the diverse backgrounds of these children. This material was personally meaningful to each of them, and it enriched their experiences as independent readers and contributed to their literary learning.

During literary discussion of a shared text, students often raise issues that lead them well beyond that text to inquiry, exploration, and discovery. For example, during a discussion of the story of Balto, several children commented that they had seen the movie about this famous sled dog. When the teacher asked them to compare the book and the movie, they identified the similarities but focused their attention on the differences. Other children who had read *Stone Fox* and had seen the movie offered to do a similar comparative analysis. This prompted a more general discussion about the differences between reading a book and watching a movie or video, as well as the changes made in film adaptations of traditional or classic titles. The day after this "detour," the teacher set up a display of single illustrated retellings of some of the traditional tales that had been adapted by Disney, such as *Beauty and the Beast, Cinderella, Aladdin,* and *Mulan.* Included in the display were the Disney adaptations in book form. The children who had seen the movies created by Disney and/or who were interested in reading retellings by writers who wished to be true to the translations of the oral tale, along with the Disney revisions written for contemporary audiences, were invited to form a small dialogue group to compare these retellings and modern revisions. Children who had recently seen Disney's *Mulan* were especially interested in comparing the book based on the movie, *Disney's Mulan* (Marsoli, 1998), and two of the retellings of this ancient tale: *The Song of Mu Lan* (Lee, 1995) and *Fa Mulan: The Story of a Woman Warrior* (San Souci, 1998). Talking about their own reading experiences in this small group setting enabled these students to gain new perspectives, to make interesting discoveries about the nature of the changes in the modern revisions, and to speculate about the reasons behind these changes.

Enriching Personal Transactions with Books: Developing Literary Awareness and Appreciation

Literary discussion of shared texts allows students to practice critical and literary thinking and to discover the understandings, interpretations, and perspectives of others. Teachers who invite their students to express differing points of view and who expect them to support, clarify, and refine or expand their initial responses to these shared texts are setting the stage for students to explore multiple meanings and study literary elements and author's craft. In the process, students build literary abilities and appreciation that will enhance their experiences as independent readers. A few examples will be presented here to illustrate the role of literary discussion in developing literary learning and helping students stretch beyond initial responses to literary texts. The ultimate goal is to provide students with literary and linguistic knowledge that will enrich their personal reading experiences.

The literary discussions that evolved during the thematic unit featuring dogs (discussed above) included a focus on authors' use of *viewpoint* in the stories selected as shared texts. The teacher introduced this literary term at the beginning of this cumulative experience and invited the students to identify the viewpoint(s) used in each shared text and in stories selected for independent reading. By the end of the unit, the students compared all the stories and explored the craft of each author and the role of viewpoint in his or her narrative. The students explored the ways authors used viewpoint as a literary technique to enable readers to enter into the inner world of a character and to share the perspective of that character. They noted that viewpoint was used to elicit sympathy for one character and to arouse negative feelings toward others. They identified the authors who told their stories from the viewpoint of the dog character to create humor. They especially enjoyed the humor created by the technique of alternating the viewpoints of human and dog:

> "A lot of the stories are about kids who are trying to train their dogs . . . but the reason *A Boy in the Doghouse* [Duffey, 1991] is so funny is because the author tells you what the boy is thinking and then in the next chapter she tells what the *dog* is thinking!"
>
> "So you get the viewpoint of *both* . . . in every other chapter. It's the same technique in *Lucky in Left Field* [Duffey, 1992]."
>
> "Another funny one is *The Adventures of Taxi Dog* [Barracca, 1990]. In that one the dog tells his *own* story about how he gets adopted by the taxi man."
>
> "*Pole Dog* [Seymour, 1993] is the dog's viewpoint, but it's not supposed to be a funny story. At first it's sad because you feel how lonely he is when his owners leave him all alone on the side of the road. I was so mad that they did that, but when that other family took him home, you just *feel* how happy he is!!"
>
> "It's like in that story about the boy who is sad when his dog disappears in the storm [*Lost in the Storm* (Carrick, 1974)]. That one is told from the boy's viewpoint; it's really the boy's story. I felt sorry for him. I knew just how he felt because my dog got lost once. . . ."
>
> "I found a wordless book. It's called *a day, a dog* [Vincent, 1999]. It's the dog's viewpoint. It's about a dog that gets left off, too. It is *really* sad."

"The one I read is called *Unknown* [Thompson, 2000]. That's the name of the dog at the pound who's sad because no one wants to take her home. But then she saves the other dogs during a fire. So she's a hero! It's her viewpoint, so you feel so happy for her at the end."

"In *Rosie: A Visiting Dog's Story* [Calmenson, 1994], the author tells about her *own* dog so you know it's a true story."

"The story that's really different is the fantasy one about the boy who got changed into a dog! It's his viewpoint . . . as a boy *and* a dog! [*The Boy Who Knew the Language of the Birds* (Wetterer, 1991)]. I got scared when he used up all three wishes and he was still a dog. . . ."

"I know. . . . I was so glad when he finally got to be a human again!"

The cumulative discussion generated by the fiction and nonfiction introduced in this literary unit also included a focus on *genre*. For example, the students noted that authors of realistic fiction created dog characters that were true to their own species. In contrast, fantasy writers created dog characters that were more like humans in behavior, language, goals, and interests. They also observed that the dogs in stories such as *Martha Speaks* (Meddaugh, 1992) were pets, but the dogs in other fantasies were central characters, as in *Gertrude, the Bulldog Detective* (Christelow, 1992) and *Deputy Shep* (Stolz, 1991). In the latter story, the dogs had pets of their own! The students talked about nonfiction texts that provided information such as characteristics of different breeds, the care and training of dogs, and the role of working dogs in the lives of humans. They noted that many of the authors of fiction had used this factual information to create their stories. One student observed: "When authors use *real facts* to make a story, then the *story* is more real. It's more believable." When these students engaged in personal reading, many of them developed the habit of identifying the genre of the material they had selected to read. Experience with different genres helps students discover their distinguishing features and understand what to expect of each genre. Students' knowledge of genre is a critical factor in their ability to generate meaning as independent readers.

Promoting, Supporting, and Nurturing the Reading Habit

There are many ways teachers promote, support, and nurture the reading habit in the classroom. The author has had opportunities to observe such teachers in their classrooms, and some of the practices used by these teachers are listed below.

Availability of High-Quality Books

These classrooms are well stocked with a wide range of high-quality literature for independent reading. These collections include diverse genres: traditional literature, modern fantasy, poetry, contemporary and historical realistic fiction, series books, short stories, biographies and autobiographies, and informational books. Students will find the works of fine authors and illustrators in these collections. The characters in these books reflect the cultural, social, and personal diversity in the classroom and in our society, so that students can find reading material that mirrors their own experiences *and* broadens their perspectives about human experience in all its diversity. The books in these collections represent a wide range of reading levels to meet the needs of prereaders, beginning readers, transition readers, and experienced readers.

Time for Browsing and Selection

Students of all ages need time to become involved in the process of selecting books for independent reading. The selection process is a social as well as a personal experience. Children are invited to talk about their choices, to exchange recommendations, and to help each other find what they would like to read.

Book Selection Assistance

Book talks by students and teachers are scheduled at regular intervals to introduce new titles and/or authors. A "best-seller" list of students' favorite books is posted and updated on a regular basis. Students who enjoy art projects create posters to "advertise" popular titles. Book clubs are established to allow students to talk about personal reading experiences in small groups. In the context of these informal conversations, children discover new titles, authors, and topics to add to their possible choices for independent reading. In several of the classrooms observed by the author, students publish a monthly newsletter that includes a book review segment.

Time for Silent Reading

A quiet reading period is scheduled into the daily routine to allow for independent reading and the pursuit of personal interests. The regularity of these quiet reading periods suggests to the children that reading is valued as a private, personal experience. Thus, books and time are made available to children so they can experience the joy of solitary transactions with books.

Reading Partners

Children are also given opportunities to read with a partner and to talk about the story as it unfolds. They may decide to work together on a project that would extend this reading experience. Although children are usually invited to choose their partners without the teacher's input, the teacher may at times ask a more experienced reader to read with a less experienced reader or with a classmate whose first language is not English.

Reading Journals

The children are invited to keep a record of the titles and authors they have selected for independent reading and to record their personal responses and interpretations. Beginning writers can choose to draw pictures about the story and dictate captions to the teacher. As they become more confident and independent as writers, the children write their own captions, and eventually they use pictures only occasionally to illustrate their prose entries. As students develop the habit of recording their responses to the texts they read, they learn about the personal nature of transactions with literary texts. And, as students review their reading records in the journal, they gain a sense of their own growth as readers. In addition to keeping an ongoing record of current reading experiences, students can record ideas or plans for future reading experiences. That is, the Reading Journal can be divided into two sections, designated as "Now" and "Later," respectively. The "Later" section is used to record items such as titles, authors, illustrators, topics, or series recommended by peers, teachers, or librarians. Students are introduced to new titles during literary discussions or book talks or in student-made posters. Students begin to look at displays of new books at local bookstores and public libraries to get ideas for independent reading. They also find suggestions for future reading in the classroom on two wall charts that are updated each month by the students: the "Best-Seller List," featuring the most popular books, and the "Best Books List," featuring the books that received the highest ratings by the students on a scale of one to ten. Students are invited to bring their Reading Journals to the library when it is time to select new books for independent reading. The "Later" list is a useful guide for making choices for new reading experiences.

Small Dialogue Groups

The literary discussion that evolves in the context of whole-group read-aloud sessions is complemented and extended in small dialogue groups in which students share responses to books they have selected from the classroom collection or school library for independent reading. These dialogue groups are formed by students who have read the same title, or different books by a single author, or books with a common theme, topic, or genre. The students share and discuss personal responses and interpretations, and they look for connections between these self-selected books and the shared texts selected by the teacher and discussed in the whole-group sessions. They enrich these informal, student-initiated dialogues by drawing from their growing store of literary understandings derived from the literary discussions of shared texts. Members of these small groups may choose to collaborate on projects that will extend their reading experiences or advertise titles they think their classmates would enjoy reading. Some groups may set up a display of favorite books, such as "Favorite Mysteries," "Favorite Fantasies," or "Favorite Horse Books."

Reading beyond the Classroom

The ultimate goal of the personalized reading program in the classroom is the development of voluntary reading habits beyond the classroom. To this end, children are invited to borrow books from the school and classroom libraries. In addition, they are encouraged to obtain library cards and to make use of their public libraries on a regular basis. Ideally, the visit to the local library becomes an integral part of the family's weekly routine. Parent meetings are scheduled to promote after-school reading and to encourage a regular read-aloud time in which parents and children share the pleasures of literary experiences. Parents are invited to organize parent-child book clubs to foster ongoing literary discussions outside the classroom.

All of the practices listed above can serve to promote, support, and nurture children's engagement and involvement in voluntary reading in and beyond the classroom. Literary discussion, the core of the literary program in elementary school classrooms, sets the stage for exposing children to a wide variety of high-quality literature, helping them to develop literary awareness and appreciation and promoting the motivation to read for personal pleasure and growth.

Children's Books Cited

Barber, Antonia, reteller. (1998). *Apollo & Daphne: Masterpieces of Greek Mythology*. [With paintings from the great art museums of the world.] Los Angeles: J. Paul Getty Museum.

Barracca, Debra, & Barracca, Sal. (1990). *The Adventures of Taxi Dog*. Illustrated by Mark Buehner. New York: Dial.

Belpré, Pura, reteller. (1978). *The Rainbow-Colored Horse*. Illustrated by Antonio Martorell. New York: Frederick Warne.

Blake, Robert J. (1997). *Akiak: A Tale from the Iditarod*. New York: Philomel.

Bushey, Jeanne. (1994). *A Sled Dog for Moshi*. Illustrated by Germaine Arnaktauyok. New York: Hyperion.

Calmenson, Stephanie. (1994). *Rosie: A Visiting Dog's Story*. Illustrated by Justin Sutcliffe. New York: Houghton Mifflin.

Carrick, Carol. (1974). *Lost in the Storm*. Illustrated by Donald Carrick. New York: Clarion.

Christelow, Eileen. (1992). *Gertrude, the Bulldog Detective*. New York: Clarion.

Climo, Shirley, reteller. (1993). *The Korean Cinderella*. Illustrated by Ruth Heller. New York: HarperCollins.

Climo, Shirley, reteller. (1995). *Atalanta's Race: A Greek Myth*. Illustrated by Alexander Koshkin. New York: Clarion.

Coburn, Jewell Rinehart. (1998). *Angkat, the Cambodian Cinderella*. Illustrated by Eddie Flotte. Auburn, CA: Shen's Books.

Coolidge, Olivia. (1952). *The Trojan War*. Illustrated by Edouard Sandoz. Boston: Houghton Mifflin.

Craft, Charlotte. (1999). *King Midas and the Golden Touch*. Illustrated by Kinuko Craft. New York: Morrow.

D'Aulaire, Ingri, & D'Aulaire, Edgar Parin. (1962). *Book of Greek Myths*. New York: Doubleday.

Duffey, Betsy. (1991). *A Boy in the Doghouse*. Illustrated by Leslie H. Morrill. New York: Simon and Schuster.

Duffey, Betsy. (1992). *Lucky in Left Field*. Illustrated by Leslie H. Morrill. New York: Simon and Schuster.

Fisher, Leonard Everett. (1988). *Theseus and the Minotaur*. New York: Holiday House.

Fisher, Leonard Everett. (1991). *Cyclops*. New York: Holiday House.

Gardiner, John Reynolds. (1980). *Stone Fox*. Illustrated by Marcia Sewall. New York: Crowell.

Hamilton, Virginia. (2000). *The Girl Who Spun Gold*. Illustrated by Leo Dillon and Diane Dillon. New York: Blue Sky Press.

Hickox, Rebecca. (1998). *The Golden Sandal: A Middle Eastern Cinderella Story*. Illustrated by Will Hillenbrand. New York: Holiday House.

Hovey, Kate, reteller. (2000). *Arachne Speaks*. Illustrated by Blair Drawson. New York: McElderry.

Hutton, Warwick. (1992). *The Trojan Horse*. New York: Macmillan.

Jaffe, Nina. (1998). *The Way Meat Loves Salt: A Cinderella Tale from the Jewish Tradition*. Illustrated by Louise August. New York: Holt.

Kellogg, Steven. (1979). *Pinkerton, Behave!* New York: Dial.

Kimmel, Elizabeth Cody. (1999). *Balto and the Great Race*. Illustrated by Nora Koerber. New York: Random House.

Kramer, S. A. (1993). *Adventure in Alaska: An Amazing True Story of the World's Longest, Toughest Dog Sled Race*. Illustrated by Karen Meyer. New York: Bullseye.

Lee, Jeanne M. (1995). *The Song of Mu Lan*. Arden, NC: Front Street.

Louie, Ai-Ling, reteller. (1982). *Yeh-Shen: A Cinderella Story from China*. Illustrated by Ed Young. New York: Philomel.

Marsoli, Lisa Ann, adapter. (1998). *Disney's Mulan*. Illustrated by Judith Clarke. Burbank, CA: MouseWorks.

Mayer, Marianna. (1998). *Pegasus*. Illustrated by Kinuko Craft. New York: Morrow.

McBratney, Sam. (1998). *Celtic Myths*. Illustrated by Stephen Player. New York: Peter Bedrick Books.

McCaughrean, Geraldine, reteller. (1998). *The Bronze Cauldron: Myths and Legends of the World*. Illustrated by Bee Willey. New York: McElderry Books.

McCaughrean, Geraldine, reteller. (1998). *Greek Gods and Goddesses*. Illustrated by Emma Chichester Clark. New York: McElderry Books.

Meddaugh, Susan. (1992). *Martha Speaks*. Boston: Houghton Mifflin.

Morley, Jacqueline. (1998). *Greek Myths*. Illustrated by Giovanni Caselli. New York: Peter Bedrick Books.

Osborne, Mary Pope. (1996). *Favorite Norse Myths*. Illustrated by Troy Howell. New York: Scholastic.

Paulsen, Gary. (1993). *Dogteam*. Illustrated by Ruth Wright Paulsen. New York: Delacorte Press.

Philip, Neil, reteller. (1996). *Odin's Family: Myths of the Vikings*. Illustrated by Maryclare Foa. New York: Orchard Books.

Philip, Neil, reteller. (1997). *The Adventures of Odysseus*. Illustrated by Peter Malone. New York: Orchard Books.

Pitre, Felix, reteller. (1995). *Paco and the Witch*. New York: Lodestar.

San Souci, Robert D., reteller. (1989). *The Talking Eggs: A Folktale from the American South*. Illustrated by Jerry Pinkney. New York: Dial.

San Souci, Robert D. (1998). *Cendrillon: A Caribbean Cinderella*. Illustrated by J. Brian Pinkney. New York: Simon & Schuster.

San Souci, Robert D., reteller. (1998). *Fa Mulan: The Story of a Woman Warrior*. Illustrated by Jean Tseng and Mou-Sien Tseng. New York: Hyperion.

Seymour, Tres. (1993). *Pole Dog*. Illustrated by David Soman. New York: Orchard.

Standiford, Natalie. (1989). *The Bravest Dog Ever: The True Story of Balto*. Illustrated by Donald Cook. New York: Random House.

Steptoe, John, reteller. (1987). *Mufaro's Beautiful Daughters: An African Tale*. New York: Lothrop, Lee & Shepard.

Stewig, John W., reteller. (1995). *Princess Florecita and the Iron Shoes: A Spanish Fairy Tale*. Illustrated by Wendy Popp. New York: Knopf.

Stewig, John W., reteller. (1999). *King Midas*. Illustrated by Omar Rayyan. New York: Holiday House.

Stolz, Mary. (1991). *Deputy Shep*. Illustrated by Pamela Johnson. New York: HarperCollins.

Sutcliff, Rosemary, reteller. (1996). *The Wanderings of Odysseus: The Story of the Odyssey*. Illustrated by Alan Lee. New York: Delacorte.

Thompson, Colin. (2000). *Unknown*. Illustrated by Anna Pignatrao. New York: Walker.

Vincent, Gabrielle. (1999). *a day, a dog*. Asheville, NC: Front Street.

Waldherr, Kris, reteller and illustrator. (1995). *The Book of Goddesses*. Hillsboro, OR: Beyond Words Publishing.

Wetterer, Margaret K. (1991). *The Boy Who Knew the Language of the Birds*. Illustrated by Beth Wright. Minneapolis: Carolrhoda.

Whelan, Gloria. (1988). *Silver*. Illustrated by Stephen Marchesi. New York: Random House.

Wood, Ted. (1996). *Iditarod Dream: Dusty and His Sled Dogs Compete in Alaska's Jr. Iditarod*. New York: Walker.

Yep, Laurence, reteller. (1997). *The Dragon Prince: A Chinese Beauty and the Beast Tale*. Illustrated by Kam Mak. New York: HarperCollills.

Yolen, Jane. (1991). *Wings*. Illustrated by Dennis Nolan. San Diego: Harcourt Brace Jovanovich.

Yolen, Jane. (1998). *Pegasus, the Flying Horse*. Illustrated by Ming Li. New York: Dutton.

Young, Ed, translator and illustrator. (1989). *Lon Po Po: A Red-Riding Hood Story from China*. New York: Philomel.

Young, Ed, reteller and illustrator. (1994). *Little Plum*. New York: Philomel.

7 Wishes and Dreams: A Thematic Literary Unit

"I like *this* story [*The Old Woman Who Lived in a Vinegar Bottle* (Godden, 1972)] better than the one we read yesterday [*The Old Woman Who Lived in a Vinegar Bottle* (MacDonald, 1995)]."

"Me too! In *this* one, the old woman is really nice. She threw the fish back in the water and she didn't even *expect* a reward. But when the fish said she could have wishes because of her kindness, she said she didn't need anything!"

"When she looked at that poor fish, I just *knew* she'd throw it back . . . like in the story we read last week: *The Fisherman and His Wife* [Grimm, 1978]. And she got wishes just like the fisherman."

"She was nice to begin with and said "thank you" to the fish. But the fisherman's wife was mean and greedy from the beginning and so was the old woman in the story yesterday. She was always complaining about her house. When the fairy came and gave her the wishes, she never said "thank you," she just wanted more."

"The big difference is that in *that* story the woman didn't even *earn* the wishes!"

"But neither did the fisherman's wife. *He's* the one who threw the fish back. He didn't even *want* the wishes even though he deserved the reward for kindness."

"But even the nice woman got greedier and greedier just like the others. And all the stories ended the same. . . . They all ended up back where they started."

"These stories are like circles. We can call them *circle tales*!"

"I don't think *this* one ended the same. The old woman said 'I'm sorry' and she stopped being selfish and greedy. *That* was different. But she did end up in the same house."

"She learned something—about herself! Remember when she said, 'I'm a greedy old woman and I didn't even know it'?"

"And you can *see* in these pictures . . . [points to relevant illustrations in the middle of the story and on the last page] how she changed back to being nice."

"And the fish wasn't mad at her anymore . . . like in the fisherman story . . . and the fish gave her a meal every Sunday, and he told her she was *still* a kind old woman . . . so it was a nicer ending."

"The fish even said she could get all the stuff back. She said no . . . just a hot dinner sometimes . . . please."

"I liked that part when the fish said he thought it was going to be a *sad* story, but it wasn't!"

"I read another one that had a good ending. It was another *Fisherman and His Wife* [Wells, 1998] story, but the characters were cats and the husband and wife were nice at first and then the fish gave them wishes for being kind and then the wife got selfish and greedy but then they changed back *themselves* and went back to their first house. So it was a circle story but it was more like *this* one."

"I think I see a pattern! The characters that started out kind and nice ended up that way because that's the way they were *inside*. But the ones that were selfish from the beginning . . . and didn't even *earn* the wishes . . . they stayed selfish and unhappy because that's how *they* were inside."

"I think it's sort of like what the fairy said in the story yesterday: 'Happiness comes from the heart, not from the house'" [unpaged].

This interchange was excerpted from a literary discussion in which a group of third graders responded to *The Old Woman Who Lived in a Vinegar Bottle* as retold by Rumer Godden, who recorded this old British folktale as it had been told in her family for four generations. The discussion evolved in the context of a thematic literary unit structured around a series of stories featuring wishes and dreams.

The Thematic Literary Unit: A Context for Literary Discussion

Most of the literary discussions described in this book served as the core of thematic literary units[1] in which children were given opportunities to enjoy and study literature in cumulative literary experiences. A thematic literary unit is organized around a central focus: a topic, genre, literary pattern, narrative element, or author. This central focus guides the selection of conceptually related texts that are used to develop a cumulative literary experience. Children are introduced to these selected texts in a series of read-aloud sessions and invited to respond to these shared texts in literary discussions, in writing, and through other forms of creative expression. Each read-aloud session begins with a discussion of the front and back covers, the endpapers, the dust jacket, and the pages preceding the first lines of the story. As the story unfolds, the children are invited to share their personal responses to the literary text and to think out loud as they engage in the meaning-making process. At the end of the story, the teacher introduces questions that build on the children's initial responses, stretch their imaginative and critical thinking, stimulate inquiry and discovery, and generate further dialogue. Through his or her own responses to the text, the teacher models active involvement as an aesthetic reader and expresses appreciation of the craft of the author and artist. Through his or her questions, the teacher demonstrates ways to study texts in terms of literary elements, the craft of authors and artists, and the use of intertextual links to generate meaning.

The stories selected for each unit are introduced in a carefully planned sequence so that each new story can be discussed in terms of those read previously. That is, reading one text serves as a preparation for reading subsequent texts. Children build a literary knowledge base from one session to the next and learn to use previous literary experiences to generate meaning as they respond to new texts. They learn to explore connections between these diverse literary texts, and the cumulative literary experience that is the core of the thematic unit takes advantage of these connections between diverse texts.

The excerpt from the literary discussion presented at the beginning of this chapter illustrates the cumulative nature of this literary experience in which children respond to each new text in light of previous texts. They use prior literary experiences to explore layers of meaning, search for connections between diverse texts, develop multiple interpretations, and achieve new understandings and insights. A primary purpose of the read-aloud sessions featured in this book is to provide *all* the children with a fund of shared literary knowledge that can be used in the collaborative construction of meaning in response to new texts introduced in this cumulative experience. In the process, students are learning to use meaning-making strategies to guide and enrich their transactions with literary texts as independent readers.

The Wishes and Dreams Unit

The thematic literary unit described in this chapter was designed for third-grade students, but it can be adapted for older or younger students. An extensive bibliography of books featuring wishes and dreams is included at the end of this chapter for teachers who would like to develop their own Wishes and Dreams unit for their students. Some of the titles in this bibliography are recent publications and were not available when the plan for this unit was initially translated into practice with third graders. With the exception of these recent publications, the titles in this bibliography were selected for the classroom collection and used for read-aloud sessions and independent reading. The focus for this unit was chosen because of the importance of wishes and dreams in the lives of young children, as well as in the lives of storybook characters. Indeed, having a wish granted and making a dream come true are typical motifs or patterns found in traditional as well as modern stories. In some of these stories, a wish is used foolishly or has unexpected or undesirable consequences. In other stories, a wish is used wisely, often to help others. In many stories, wishes are granted in return for a kind and generous deed. In most, central characters learn something from their experiences, and the reader or listener learns something about human nature.

The focus of this thematic literary unit provided the basis for selecting a series of books that were introduced and discussed during the read-aloud sessions and for building a classroom collection of thematically related books for independent reading. The teacher selected books that represent various literary genres, that include characters who represent diverse backgrounds, and that address important themes or significant truths about the human experience. The books intended for independent reading included a wide range of literary material to meet the various interests and literary/literacy experience and skills of the children involved. The children were invited to choose one or more titles to read independently during the quiet periods structured into the daily schedule for solitary reading or for reading with a partner. They were also able to take the books home to share with family members. The children were encouraged to search for connections between their self-selected books and the shared texts discussed during the group read-aloud sessions and to contribute their findings to the literary discussions. For example, in this chapter's opening segment, one child identified an interesting connection between his self-selected book, Rosemary Wells's adaptation of *The Fisherman and His Wife* (1998), and the shared text, Rumer Godden's retelling of the British variant of this fairy tale, *The Old Woman Who Lived in a Vinegar Bottle* (1972).

Objectives

The objectives that were developed to guide the planning of the Wishes and Dreams unit are listed below. As the plans for this unit were translated into practice, these objectives guided the ongoing evaluation of the children's strengths and weaknesses and their involvement as aesthetic and critical readers, as students of literature, and as participants in the cumulative literary discussions. This ongoing evaluation process informed the translation of the plan into practice by highlighting the elements of the original plan that needed revision in order to meet the needs of the children. At the conclusion of the unit, the objectives provided points of reference for assessing the children's learning as well as the relative success of the literary unit as a teaching/learning experience. These objectives (which are referred to by number in various places throughout this chapter) were:

1. To provide opportunities for children to engage in enjoyable experiences with literature.

2. To provide a context for studying literary themes illuminating the human experience in stories featuring wishes and dreams and for exploring connections between literature and life.

3. To provide opportunities for children to develop the motivation, knowledge, and strategies necessary to become active and thoughtful readers who explore books on their own.

4. To provide opportunities for children to engage in comparative analysis of multiple texts, to use intertextual links to generate meaning, and to learn to respond to each new story in light of previous texts.

5. To provide opportunities for children to learn about literature, literary elements, the language of literary analysis, and the craft of storytellers, authors, and artists.

6. To provide opportunities for children to draw from their growing knowledge about literature and author's craft to compose original narratives.

7. To provide literary experiences in which children are challenged to stretch their minds and imaginations and to engage in lively discussions stimulated by inquiry, discovery, and the "cover-to-cover" study of literary texts.

8. To provide opportunities for students to respond to literature and to share their thoughts, feelings, interpretations, questions, and discoveries in oral discussions, personal journals, original narratives, and other forms of creative expression.

9. To provide opportunities for children to learn to work together and to form a community of readers in which they explore and build meanings together.

10. To provide experiences with diverse literary genres, including traditional and modern tales, fantasy and realism, and nonfiction.

11. To provide opportunities for children to learn about the relationships between traditional and modern literature as well as modern writers' use of the oral tradition to create new stories.

12. To provide experiences with literature that reflects the diversity in our schools and in our pluralistic society and that offers a context for building a global perspective.

13. To provide a context for independent reading and writing and to encourage transition readers to move into longer stories or chapter books.

14. To provide opportunities for children to discover new possibilities for developing and expanding personal reading interests.

Introducing Diverse Genres: The Read-Aloud Sessions and Independent Reading

Several traditional tales were presented in the initial read-aloud sessions to introduce the focus of this thematic unit: wishes and dreams. *The Fisherman and His Wife* (Grimm, 1978) and the two versions of *The Old Woman Who Lived in a Vinegar Bottle* mentioned earlier were read aloud in the first three sessions. In subsequent sessions, the children listened to and discussed other traditional tales from different cultures: *The Three Wishes: An Old Story* (Zemach, 1986), a French fairy tale; *Liang and the Magic Paintbrush* (Demi, 1980), a Chinese folktale; *Gluskabe and the Four Wishes* (Bruchac, 1995), an Abenaki Indian tale; *The Spirit of the Blue Light* (Mayer, 1990), a German fairy tale; *King Midas and the Golden Touch* (Craft, 1999), a tale from Greek mythology; *The Tale of Aladdin and His Wonderful Lamp: A Story from the Arabian Nights* (Kimmel, 1992); and *The Story of Jumping Mouse* (Steptoe, 1984), a Plains Indian tale. (See Objectives 10 and 12.)

The books selected for independent reading included adaptations and retellings of traditional tales. For example, *Rosa & Marco and the Three Wishes* (Brenner, 1992) is a modern adaptation of *The Three Wishes* for beginning readers; *Sydney Rella and the Glass Sneaker* (Myers, 1985) is a modern revision of the Cinderella tale for beginning readers; *Sleeping Ugly* (Yolen, 1981) is a modern revision of the tale of Sleeping Beauty for beginning readers; *Tye May and the Magic Brush* (Bang, 1981) is an adaptation of the old Chinese folktale for beginning readers; and *Aladdin and the Magic Lamp* (Hautzig, 1993), is an adaptation of this old tale from *The Arabian Nights* for beginning readers. Single illustrated retellings of traditional tales included in the collection of books for independent reading were: *King Midas and the Golden Touch* (Hewitt, 1987); *King Midas* (Stewig, 1999); *The Magic Wings: A Tale from China* (Wolkstein, 1983); *The Three Wishes* (Galdone, 1961), another retelling of this old English fairy tale; *A Tale of Three Wishes* (Singer, 1976), an old Jewish tale; and *Yeh-Shen: A Cinderella Story from China* (Louie, 1982) and *Wishbones: A Folk Tale from China* (Wilson, 1993), both ancient Chinese variants of the Cinderella tale. Two illustrated editions of Grimm tales, *The Glass Mountain* (1985) and *The Seven Ravens* (1994), chronicle the consequences of thoughtless wishes uttered in moments of frustration and anger. In both stories, the parents had never intended their wishes to come true, but their own children were transformed into ravens the moment the wish passed their lips.

Several modern fairy tales were presented in the read-aloud sessions to introduce another genre to the children: *The Moon's Revenge* (Aiken, 1987); *Chickpea and the Talking Cow* (Glass, 1987); two versions of *Greyling* (Yolen, 1968, 1991); and *The Boy Who Knew the Language of the Birds* (Wetterer, 1991). Modern fairy tales selected for the independent reading collection included "Bridget's Hat" (Aiken, 1978); "The Wind Cap" (Yolen, 1977); *One Big Wish* (Williams, 1980), a tall tale; *Do Not Open* (Turkle, 1981); *Juma and the Magic Jinn* (Anderson, 1986), a fairy tale fantasy embedded in a realistic tale set in Kenya; and *Tico and the Golden Wings* (Lionni, 1964).

Picture storybooks were introduced in the final group of read-aloud sessions: *Burnt Toast on Davenport Street* (Egan, 1997), a humorous animal fantasy; *Big Boy* (Mollel, 1995), a fantasy adventure embedded in a realistic story set in Africa; *Barney Bipple's Magic Dandelions* (Chapman, 1977), a tall tale illustrated by Steven Kellogg; and *The Dream Jar* (Pryor, 1996), a realistic story.

Picture storybooks selected for independent reading included five animal fantasies—*Mordant's Wish* (Coursen, 1997), *Fritz and the Beautiful Horses* (Brett, 1981), *I Wish I Were a Butterfly* (Howe, 1987), *Perfect the Pig* (Jeschke, 1980), and *Jubal's Wish* (Wood, 2000); *Fanny's Dream* (Buehner, 1996), a realistic tale with a Cinderella element; *Three Wishes* (Clifton, 1992), a realistic story of friendship shaped by the "three wishes" motif; *The Magic Bicycle* (Doherty, 1995), a realistic story of a young boy who dreams of riding a two-wheel bicycle; *Bright Star* (Crew, 1997), a realistic story of a girl who wishes for the freedom to follow her own dreams; *Mirette on the High Wire (McCully, 1992)*, a realistic story set in Paris one hundred years ago; *The Dandelion Wish* (Horn, 2000), another realistic story; and *Whoosh! Went the Wish* (Speed, 1997), a fantasy with a surprise ending.

The books selected for independent reading also included reading material to meet the needs of children who had advanced beyond books for beginning readers and picture storybooks. These young readers were ready for the challenges inherent in early chapter books, such as *The Trouble with Wishes* (Pfeffer, 1996), *Beany (Not Beanhead) and the Magic Crystal* (Wojciechowski, 1997), *Ark in the Park* (Orr, 2000), *My Dog, Cat* (Crisp, 2000), *The Wish Giver* (Brittain, 1983), *A Magic Crystal?* (a Marvin Redpost story) by Louis Sachar (2000), and *I Was a Rat!* (Pullman, 2000). (See Objective 13.)

Nonfiction texts in the independent-reading collection added another dimension to the children's experience with stories of wishes and dreams. For example, several picture book biographies were included to introduce the children to remarkable individuals who managed to make their own dreams come true. *Zora Hurston and the Chinaberry Tree* (Miller, 1994) is a lyrical account of a childhood episode in the life of this well-known African American writer whose mother taught her to follow her dreams. *The Boy Who Loved to Draw: Benjamin West* (Brenner, 1999) is the life story of a boy who spent all his time drawing and dreamed of becoming a painter. Today he is known as the first world-famous American artist. *Happy Birthday, Martin Luther King* (Marzollo, 1993) is a brief introduction to the great civil rights leader who shared his dream with a quarter of a million people in Washington, D.C., in 1963. *Wilma Unlimited: How Wilma Rudolph Became the World's Fastest Woman* (Krull, 1996) is a biography of the African American woman who overcame crippling polio as a child to become the first woman to win three gold medals in track in a single Olympics.

Other biographies in the independent-reading collection were selected to meet the needs of children ready for early chapter books. For example, *Lynette Woodard: The First Female Globetrotter* (Rosenthal, 1986) is the story of the first woman to play basketball with the Harlem Globetrotters. She had dreamed of being part of this team since she was five years old. Her dream came true in 1985 after years of hard work and a remarkable career as a basketball player. *Jim Henson: From Puppets to Muppets* (Woods, 1987) is the life story of the puppeteer whose creations have entertained millions of people around the world. His dream was to work in television, and at age sixteen he got a job working as a puppeteer at a local station; he had taken his first step toward realizing his dream. *Babe Didrikson: Athlete of the Century* (Knudson, 1985) focuses on the early years of Babe Didrikson Zaharias who had wanted to be a famous athlete from the time she was a young girl. Because of her athletic skill, the boys in her neighborhood gave her the nickname "Babe" after their home-run hero, Babe Ruth. Another biography of this famous athlete was included in the collection for beginning readers: *Babe Didrikson Zaharias: All-Around Athlete* (Sutcliffe, 2000).

Independent Reading, Journals, Dialogue Groups, and Extension Projects

The children recorded their responses to their independent reading experiences in reading journals. Their entries in these journals included personal feelings and opinions, insights and interpretations, and questions raised during the reading experience. The children were also encouraged to search for and record connections between these self-selected texts and the shared texts introduced in the read-aloud sessions. They were invited to share these discoveries in the literary discussions in these whole-group sessions. Questions introduced by the teacher during these group sessions were designed to encourage "cover-to-cover" reading and to call attention to genre, literary elements, story patterns, and the craft of the authors and artists who created the stories that were read aloud. The children were encouraged to use these questions as a basis for generating meaning as they read independently and recorded their personal and critical/analytical responses in their reading journals. They were expected to support their interpretations with evidence from the text or illustrations in the book they had selected for independent reading.

In the context of this cumulative literary experience, the reading journal became a running record of reader response, meaning making, and analysis and served as a vehicle for the teacher to learn about her students as thinkers, readers, and writers. Students were also invited to bring their journals to small dialogue groups that were formed to allow three to six children to meet informally to discuss particular stories and/or poems they had selected to read independently. The children in these small groups often initiated the dialogue by reading a journal entry about the story, such as a personal response, a question, a discovery, or an interpretation. (See Objectives 4, 5, 8, and 13.)

The members of each dialogue group were invited to collaborate on projects that would extend literary experiences through drama, storytelling, poetry, art activities, or research. Some groups chose to work on extension projects about a favorite text introduced in the read-aloud sessions; others chose to extend independent reading experiences. For example, the members of one group had read and discussed biographies about individuals who had made their own dreams come true. They decided to do some library research to find out more about these interesting people and to use their findings to put together their own book of word portraits of these real-life heroes and heroines. The members of a second group were interested in the ways different artists illustrated the story of King Midas. After examining and discussing the work of diverse artists in single illustrated editions of this Greek myth, as well as in collections of myths and legends, the children produced their own interpretation of this ancient tale in the form of a mural. The members of another group created an illustrated Wishing Dictionary that included the various wish givers in the stories selected for this unit, as well as the results of a survey of the responses of classmates and relatives to questions about conditions, procedures, and formulae associated with wishing. Yet another group focused on poetry about wishes and dreams (see the poetry list at the end of this chapter). After sharing, comparing, and interpreting the poems they found in diverse collections, the children decided to put together their own collection of "Wish and Dream Poems" in an illustrated book. Their book included both the work of professional poets and original poems they had been inspired to create on their own.

Cumulative Literary Discussions in the Read-Aloud Sessions

Three traditional tales were selected to introduce the thematic literary unit featuring stories about wishes and dreams. As each new tale was read aloud, the title was recorded on a wall chart. The literary discussion in the opening segment of this chapter was drawn from the third read-aloud session in this cumulative experience. The children shared their personal responses to Rumer Godden's retelling of *The Old Woman Who Lived in a Vinegar Bottle* and then analyzed it in terms of the stories read aloud in the first two sessions. The child who found a connection between these shared texts and the book he had selected to read independently introduced this fourth title into the comparative analysis. Thus, in the context of this cumulative discussion, the children had begun to use intertextual links to generate meaning as they focused on character, plot, and theme development, as well as on the structure of the stories. This dialogue also revealed the children's use of text and illustrations to support their observations and interpretations of a specific book. (See Objective 4.)

Before reading another traditional tale in the fourth group session, the teacher asked the children: "Have you ever made a wish? Tell us about it." Every child had something to share in response to this question. The children talked about making wishes on the first star of evening, before blowing out birthday candles or blowing on a dandelion puff, in their bedtime prayers, and by tossing pennies into fountains and wishing wells. They recited or chanted poems and special formulae and rules that were part of the wishing process. Many told personal stories of a wish that came true. While for some these experiences served to confirm their belief in the powers of magic, Santa Claus, the tooth fairy, or wishing wells, for others these experiences had logical and rational explanations. One child observed, "When you wish for a special toy or something, your mom and dad can usually grant the wish, but if you wish you didn't have allergies or freckles—well, they can't do that." Another child added, "Or if you wish you can fly—*that* kind of wish is only granted in stories." A third child argued, "But I wished for a baby sister, and that's just what we got!" The first child replied, "But your wish didn't *make* it a girl. That's from the genes or something. But in a *story*, you can wish for a baby even if you're not pregnant! That's what happened in 'Tom Thumb.'" Most of the children nodded in agreement when a fourth child stated, "Well I just make wishes anyway, because they *could* come true. I mean you never know."

At the conclusion of the children's conversation about wishing, the teacher pointed to the bookshelves with the large collection of books selected for this cumulative literary experience (see list of titles at the end of this chapter). She asked the children to think about why so many storytellers long ago as well as so many modern authors have chosen to create stories and poems about wishes and dreams. (See Objective 2.) A few of their responses to this question are recorded below:

> "I guess most people *make* wishes, so they would like stories about wishes. . . ."
>
> "That's probably why storytellers make up wishing stories—because even though the stories have magic, wishes are real—I mean in real life."
>
> "That's right. That's just what we were talking about! Everybody makes wishes so that's why it's in so many stories."

At this point the teacher showed the children the other old stories she planned to read aloud and reminded them about the nature of these "retold tales." She talked about the way these stories from diverse cultures around the world were transformed as they were passed on orally from storyteller to storyteller across centuries and continents before they were recorded and retold. She showed the children how to identify "retold tales" and invited them to look through the collection to find other traditional tales. These children had been learning about the Dewey decimal classification system used in most school and public libraries, and they were delighted to discover the significance of the number "398" on the spines of the traditional tales and on the shelves in the nonfiction section of the library. One child responded to this discovery with, "So *that's* where all the good stories are!"

Before reading aloud *The Three Wishes* (Zemach, 1986), the teacher asked the children to use the front cover to make predictions about the content of the story:

"The man and lady on the cover look sort of poor, so they'll probably wish for riches."

"They look nice. You can tell by their faces and the way they're petting the dog."

"But who do you think will *give* them the three wishes?"

"Maybe the dog is magic and they were nice to it? Remember that story about Shiro, the little white dog that rewarded the old man and lady who were so nice to it?"[2]

As the story unfolded, the children were able to answer their own questions and to confirm or revise their predictions. For example, after the scene of the rescue of the imp, one child interjected: "That answers Jim's question. The imp is the wish giver!"

At the conclusion of the story, the children initiated a comparative analysis in which they explored connections between this story and the previously shared stories as well as stories they had selected from the collection to read independently at school or at home.

"This one's like the others. . . . The man and his wife rescue the imp, and the fisherman in the first story and that nice old woman in the third story let the fish live and they all got rewarded with wishes." [This child pointed to the story titles listed on the chart next to the story circle.]

"And when they helped them, they didn't *know* they'd get wishes. I think that's important."

"You're right, Kristin! That's how you know they're doing it because they're *kind*. So they get rewarded for their kindness."

"And it's just the *opposite* for the greedy, selfish people like the fisherman's wife. She didn't *earn* the wishes so in the end she *didn't* get what she wanted!"

"I read another retold story almost exactly like this, but the woodcutter found a little tree fairy who asked him not to cut down the tree so he didn't, and he got three wishes [*The Three Wishes*, illustrated by Paul Galdone (1961)]."

"I read that, too. They all made foolish wishes and had to use the last one to undo the second one!"

"Can I have that next?"

"Sure. But some of the words are hard, though."

"I read a *new* story like this called *Rosa & Marco and the Three Wishes* [Brenner, 1992]. A boy lets a fish go free and gets three wishes and he wants a taco and his sister is mad and wishes the taco on his nose and then the last wish is to get it off his nose . . . like the sausage in the other stories."

"In this one, the imp told them to *wish wisely*. It's like a warning . . . like in Cinderella and you *know* they're not going to remember it."

"In my book there's a warning, too. A boy does a good deed and gets wishes and he's told to 'stick to simple wishes' but he does *complicated* wishes and really gets in trouble [*Barney Bipple's Magic Dandelions* (Chapman, 1977)]."

"I read *The Trouble with Wishes* [(Pfeffer, 1996)] about a girl who does a good deed, and a magic lamp gives her three wishes. And the lamp gives *her* a warning, too: 'Think before you wish' [p. 25]."

"I read that too. It's a *really* good book. Katie's first wish was a selfish one and the second wish was to undo the *damage*. But her third wish was an *unselfish* one and it helped her whole class!"

"I read an old one with my mom that's sort of like this one. It's called *A Tale of Three Wishes* [(Singer, 1975)] and in the *first part* these three kids waste their wishes instead of wishing for what they really dreamed of—just like in this story. When the girl wishes for a blintz, her brother wishes that she'd *turn into* a blintz! Then their friend uses the last wish to turn her back. But in the *second* part of the story, they grow up and they make their own dreams come true."

The children continued their comparative analysis as they listened to and discussed the other traditional tales read aloud in subsequent group sessions. They identified recurring patterns, character types, and themes in these tales. For example, they found the warning pattern in the Chinese tale, *Liang and the Magic Paintbrush* (Demi, 1980), and in the Abenaki tale, *Gluskabe and the Four Wishes* (Bruchac, 1995). They found the reward-for-kindness theme in the German tale *The Spirit of the Blue Light* (Mayer, 1990), in the Greek myth *King Midas and the Golden Touch* (Craft, 1999), and in the Plains Indian tale *The Story of Jumping Mouse* (Steptoe, 1984). They discovered interesting helper characters: the mysterious stranger in Craft's *King Midas;* the old man on the phoenix in the story of Liang; the cranky old man in *The Spirit of the Blue Light;* the great hero, Gluskabe, in the Abenaki tale; Magic Frog and the other animals Mouse meets on his quest journey in *The Story of Jumping Mouse;* and the genie of the ring and the genie of the lamp in the story of Aladdin. When the teacher read Bruchac's dedication in *Gluskabe and the Four Wishes,* the children observed that it seemed to apply to most of the stories they had already heard or read about wishing. Bruchac dedicated this book to the "Abenaki elders who teach the best wishes are unselfish ones." The children asked the teacher to write these words on the chart next to the story circle. They decided to "see how many of the wishing tales had this lesson." (See Objectives 5 and 7.)

By the fourth session in this cumulative literary experience, the children were beginning to direct their comments to each other instead of only to the teacher. They were listening to the ideas their classmates contributed to the discussion and responded to these ideas in an ongoing give-and-take. That is, this group of individual children had gradually become a community of readers exploring and building meanings together in genuine dialogue. In addition, as the children introduced their self-selected stories into the discussion in order to share the intertextual links they had found, other children in the group were often motivated to select these titles for independent reading. Peer recommendations proved to be important factors informing children's choices for independent reading. (See Objectives 9 and 14.)

In the next series of group sessions, the teacher read aloud several modern fairy tales. This time, the children spontaneously examined the covers, title page, endpapers, and dedication page of each book to make predictions about the content and then confirmed or revised these predictions as the story unfolded. As they listened to each narrative, they found recurring patterns that enabled them to "predict their way" through the story. They responded to each new story in light of previous tales they had heard in these group sessions or read independently, and they searched for intertextual links to generate meaning. They examined the illustrations to discover clues provided by the artist that were unavailable in the text. They considered each story in terms of the "wishing lesson" derived from Bruchac's dedication. For example, in *The Moon's Revenge* (Aiken, 1987), a young boy wishes to be the best fiddler in the country. The children identified this as a selfish wish, but they noted that at the end of the story he risked his own life to save the townspeople from a monster by using the special skill for which he had wished. *Chickpea and the Talking Cow* (Glass, 1987) is about a farmer's tiny son who wishes he could help his father. The children agreed that this was "an unselfish wish because it was a wish to help someone else." They also noted that Chickpea, the tiny boy, was "just like Tom Thumb!" The children especially enjoyed the Irish tale *The Boy Who Knew the Language of the Birds* (Wetterer, 1991), about a young boy who becomes the storyteller for the royal family and a spoiled princess who is given three wishes. She uses the first wish thoughtlessly, causing the transformation of the boy into a dog. When there is only one wish left, the dog/boy chooses to use it to rescue the three kidnapped princes and return them to the palace instead of using the wish to change himself back into a human. The children decided that it would take a great deal of courage to make such an unselfish wish!

Several children shared their thoughts about the modern fairy tales they had selected to read independently:

> "I read *Tico and the Golden Wings* [Lionni, 1964]. Tico was a bird who needed wings. He was sort of like Liang who needed a paint-

brush. They both got their wishes. Tico got golden wings from the wishingbird, and Liang got a magic paintbrush from the old man on the phoenix."

"I read that, too. Tico gave his gold feathers away to help people. That was unselfish. Liang was the same. He used his magic brush to make things for the poor people."

"In my story—'Bridget's Hat' [Aiken, 1978]—Bridget is a really nice character, too. She gets rewarded for her kindness to the King of the Grasshoppers! And she uses her wish to help her in her job so she can earn money to take care of her twin brother. But *he* is lazy and selfish and stole her magic wishing boots. In the end he got what he deserved! It's like the old stories!"

"The one I read, *Juma and the Magic Jinn* [Anderson, 1986], is about a selfish wish. It's about a boy who opens a blue jar and a genie comes out. But when his wishes come true, it's not what he wants! He didn't like school work and wished he could go someplace that didn't have schools, but when he *got* his wish he learned that it's important to go to school and learn new things."

"That sounds like the old story about the woodcutter and his wife. After their three wishes they learned how happy they were together even *without* all the stuff they thought of wishing for."

"And it was the same with the Vinegar Bottle lady. After the wishes, she learned how happy she was to begin with!"

"But the fisherman's wife didn't learn *anything*. I think she was just too selfish to learn to appreciate anything."

"King Midas learned from his wish, too! I think his wish was the most *selfish* of all! But he learned that love is better than gold!"

[Teacher:] "Where do you think the authors of these modern fairy tales got their ideas?" [See Objectives 2 and 11.]

"It seems like they got a lot of their ideas from the old stories . . . the retold tales."

"That's right! I read a long book with my dad, and it's like a sequel to Cinderella. It's called *I Was a Rat!* [Pullman, 2000]. The author took that part in the Cinderella story when Cinderella wishes to go to the palace ball and the fairy godmother makes her wish come true. But *this* story is what happens *after* the wish is granted! The whole story is about what happens to the *rat* that got changed into a page boy when the fairy godmother did the magic!"

"The author of 'Bridget's Hat' used a lot of the same patterns that were in the old stories, too."

By this point in the cumulative literary experience, the children were able to distinguish between traditional and modern tales and were becoming increasingly aware of modern writers' use of the oral tradition to create new stories. In the final group of read-aloud sessions, the children were introduced to picture storybooks. They were invited to focus on differences between fantasy and realism as literary genres and on the way some modern writers embed fantasy adventures in realistic stories. (See Objective 10.)

Burnt Toast on Davenport Street (Egan, 1997), an animal fantasy, is the story of Arthur and Stella, two dogs whose lives change when a fly comes in through the window and says to Arthur, "If you don't kill me, I'll grant you three wishes" (unpaged). The children were delighted to discover this story pattern from the oral tradition in a very humorous modern tale. *Big Boy* (Mollel, 1995), set in Africa, is the story of Oli, who wants to be big enough to go hunting with his older brother. When a magical bird grants him his wish to be as big as a giant, he discovers that wishes that come true often bring more than one bargains for. The children identified this tale as a fantasy adventure within a realistic story. They compared *Big Boy* with *Barney Bipple's Magic Dandelions* (Chapman, 1977):

> "They're both realistic stories with fantasy *in* them. Oli has a magical bird, and Barney is given three magic dandelions. But the stories start out in real life."
>
> "And their wishes are like real-life wishes. . . . Oli wants to be bigger so he can hunt with his brother, and Barney wants to be two years older so the older kids will play with him."
>
> "That's what I would wish . . . because my sister always says 'You're too young' whenever I want to do something with her!"
>
> "When they get their wishes . . . *that's* when the fantasy part starts."
>
> "Oli's story is more serious and the ending is real, but Barney's story is funny and the ending couldn't really happen because he gets more wishes and they all come true . . . like *everything* you'd want!"
>
> "Steven Kellogg did the pictures for Barney's story so that's why it's so funny."

When *The Dream Jar* (Pryor, 1996) was read aloud, the children identified it as a realistic story. This is the story of Valentina and her family, who have emigrated from Russia to America. Her father's dream is to own his own store. Valentina wants to contribute to their "dream jar" but her family says she is too little to help and that she must stay in school. But Valentina finds a way to earn money for the jar. She sets up a night school in their kitchen and teaches English to their neighbors. In time, she is able to help make their dream come true.

The children responded thoughtfully to this story of the immigrant experience, and they discussed it in comparison with the other stories they had heard or read:

> "She reminded me of Oli. Everyone said she's too little . . . just like him."

"I liked the way she just didn't give up. Even though she was little, *she* knew English and the adults didn't because they couldn't go to school."

"This story is like the one I read with my mom—*A Tale of Three Wishes*. The first part of the story is fantasy, but the next part is realism. That's when the three children grow up and work hard to make their own dreams come true . . . like Valentina worked hard to help her dad make his dream come true—*without* magic! In my book, when they wasted their wishes, an old man tells them you can only get what you want by *effort*. At the end, he comes back and rewards them for their effort . . . but the last part seems like fantasy again."

"The story I read—*Mirette on the High Wire* (McCully, 1992)—is like *The Dream Jar*, too. It's a realism story about a girl who dreams of becoming a tightrope artist like her friend, Mr. Bellini, and she makes her own wish come true because she works really hard and practices a lot and pays attention to what Mr. Bellini tells her."

"I read a nonfiction story like that. It's about Lynette Woodard. Her dream came true like Mirette's because she worked so hard!"

"I read another realism story. It's fiction. It's called *Three Wishes* [Clifton, 1992]. This girl finds a lucky penny and makes wishes and she thinks the wishes come true because of the magic penny but it was just a coincidence."

"I read that, too. But I think the penny *was* magic! I think it was a fantasy *in* a realism story."

At this point in their discussion, the other children asked the teacher to read this story aloud so they could enter into the debate. This story is about a friendship between an African American boy and girl, Victor and Zenobia. When Nobie finds a penny with her birthday year on New Year's Day, she knows that this is a lucky penny and that she can make three wishes. When she and Victor talk about the penny, a few thoughtless words cause angry feelings. When Zenobia says, "Man, I wish you would get out of here" (unpaged), Victor runs out of the house. As Zenobia reflects on the experiences they have shared and on what a good friend Victor is, she makes another wish: "Wish I still had a good friend." It is at this point that Victor appears, grinning at Zenobia. At the conclusion of the story, the children took up the debate about genre: Was this a realistic story with a fantasy sequence in which magic caused the wishes to come true or was it a realistic story without magical intervention?

"I think Victor just forgot about it and came over to play like nothing happened."

"Or maybe *he* had been thinking about it too and decided he wanted to be friends again, too. I don't think he'd just *forget* about it."

"I know how Zenobia felt when he left. She really missed him. But it *was* like her wish came true. He just came back! That part just didn't seem real. It was more like magic. That's not the way things happen in real life."

"But it could have been a coincidence . . . like when the sun came out after her first wish. Remember she wished it wasn't so cold? I think he just changed his mind at the same time she made the wish."

"Maybe the author just wanted to show how important friends are. Remember when her mom told her that if *she* had a wish she'd wish for good friends. She said that's what the world needs!"

At the end of their lively discussion about this book, the children were unable to reach a consensus about the genre: some continued to identify the story as realism; others identified it as a realistic story about friendship embedded with a fantasy sequence. However, their focus on genre continued when several children shared the chapter books they had read independently. For example, a number of children had selected to read *The Wish Giver* (Brittain, 1983), a story about three young people whose lives are changed when a strange man comes to town selling wishes. The narrator comments: "He earned his livelihood by selling little white cards and incredible dreams" (p. 16). One of the children brought the book to the circle to read specific segments:

"This story is realistic at first because the town and people seem real, but the fantasy part starts when the strange man comes and sells the wishing cards. He gives a *warning* like in the old stories. [At this point the boy read aloud from the text. He had written the relevant page numbers in a journal entry in which he identified intertextual links along with textual support for the connections.] 'Take great care when you wish. For it will be granted exactly as you ask for it' [p. 14]."

"I read that too. You can tell the fantasy part because there's a lot of magic! When three of them used their wishing cards, their wishes came true but *not* in the way they expected! But they finally thought of a way to get *out* of the trouble their wishes got them *in*."

"I thought of it before they did! The man at the store had the fourth card! It's the guy who tells the story, and he says, 'Maybe they'd learned a few things from what happened when they'd wished unwisely, but I'd rather tell my story and leave the teaching to others' [p. 171]. He has to figure out a way to make *one wish* to help all *three* of them. But this story is like the old ones, because the characters *learn* things about themselves and they change . . . like King Midas and the old woman in the vinegar bottle." [She pointed to Godden's retelling of this tale listed on the chart.]

After identifying the genre of *The Wish Giver* as a blend of contemporary realism and fantasy, and after discussing some of the recurring patterns that reflected its roots in traditional literature, these young readers had inspired a number of their classmates to select this title for independent reading. For some, it was a significant challenge, but their enjoyment of this humorous tale enabled them to rise to the challenge! (See Objectives 3, 13, and 14.)

Composing New Wish Tales

After listening to, reading, discussing, and writing about the stories selected for this cumulative literary experience, the children were invited to compose their own wish/dream tales. In preparation for the composing process, the teacher initiated a review of the stories read aloud in the group sessions in terms of the following considerations: genre; central characters; wish givers or helpers; antagonists or villains; the nature of the wishes; the consequences of the wishes; recurring patterns or motifs; and implied lessons, messages, or themes. The stories written by the children reflected their grasp of the literary concepts and themes about human nature explored in this cumulative literary experience. (See Objective 6.) Some children created folktales; others created realistic narratives. Almost every child clearly identified the setting, the central character, the wish giver [the realistic tales did not include this character], warnings, the nature and consequences of the wishes, and the problem and solution. Most of the stories were developed around a central theme, such as kindness rewarded and greed punished, the undesirable consequences of selfish or foolish wishes, the power of unselfish wishes, life lessons learned, or making one's own dreams come true. Many of the stories reflected the children's growing familiarity with the language of literature; some of the phrases in their stories echoed the language of traditional tales. Two examples of the "kindness rewarded" stories written by third graders are included below:

The Broken Wing

Once upon a time there was a man and his wife. The one thing they wanted was a child. Now one day the woman set out to pick blackberries for their supper. On the way she found a little bird with a broken wing. She picked him up and carefully put him in her basket. She took him home to take care of him. When she got home her husband said, "Did you get the blackberries?" "No, dear," said the woman. "This poor little bird needs us more than we need blackberries." So they both took care of the little bird and his wing got better. The man and woman were happy that the bird was well, but they were sad that the bird could fly away from them now. The next morning, the bird sang for the first time and then it talked! The bird said: "I am the king of all the birds. You have saved my life. In return for your kindness I will grant you one wish." The man and woman immediately said together: "Our wish is for a child!" The little bird said: "Look behind you." And they looked and there was a beautiful little baby! And the bird stayed with the man and his wife and their child for the rest of their lives. And they all lived happily ever after. The end.

The Horse and What His Wish Was

Once upon a time there was a horse. He did not have a tail. He wished he did. Well, one day the horse went out to go grazing. He saw something in the tall grass. He went closer. It was a small rabbit. But the rabbit didn't hop away. Then the horse saw what the problem was. The rabbit was bleeding. The horse licked the rabbit until it stopped bleeding. When the rabbit was all right, it hopped all around the horse. Then the rabbit looked up at the big horse and said, "Thank you my friend for what you did. The other animals saw me but they did not stop to help me. But you did. So I will give you a wish!" The horse was very surprised. The horse thought. Then he said, "Are you a magic rabbit?" "Yes, I am," said the rabbit. "Well then," said the horse. "I would really like to have a tail. That is my wish." "Very well," said the rabbit. "Your wish is granted!" Then, all of a sudden, the rabbit disappeared! The horse looked all around for the little rabbit. He did not see him. But he did see his lovely new tail! And that is how the horse got his wish. The end.

After the children had completed their stories, the teacher invited them to illustrate them and then to write about this creative experience in their journals. For example, she suggested that they reflect on the sources of their ideas for their stories and/or for their illustrations. The child who wrote the first story recorded these thoughts in his journal:

> I thought of the king of the birds from the king of the grasshoppers who fell in the soup in Bridget's Hat [Aiken, 1978]. I thought maybe the birds could have a king too. A nice bird. Like a dove. Bridget helped the grasshopper but she didn't know it was magic. So that's how my story is because I like it when people do nice things just because they're nice. I also thought about The Wind Cap [Yolen, 1977] and how the boy helped the turtle. But it was really a fairy and it granted his wish. But I wanted my bird to stay with them so he didn't change into a fairy. But he could talk.

When this child shared his story in the Authors' Session, he also shared this journal entry. The children responded to his original story with the same kinds of predictions and thoughtful comments that characterized their responses to the work of professional writers. The children also responded to his journal entry about this story:

> "I liked the way you explained how you got your ideas."
>
> "I got an idea from 'Bridget's Hat,' too. But I made a character like her awful brother! And I liked the pictures in 'Bridget's Hat' so I did those cutout pictures with black paper[3] for my story like in that book."
>
> "You were thinking about *different* stories and that's how you got a lot of good ideas for your story."
>
> "That's what the real authors did. Like the one who wrote the story of Rosa and Marco got her ideas from that old story *The Three Wishes.* And the one who wrote *Chickpea and the Talking Cow* must have read the story of 'Tom Thumb'!"
>
> "My story is about a girl who gives away her wish to some-one who needs it. I got the idea from *Beany [Not Beanhead] and the Magic Crystal* [Wojciechowski, 1997] when Beany gave her magic crystal to the sad old lady next door. That story was a realism story because I don't think the crystal was *really* magic. But my story was fantasy because the girl gets a wish from a wishingbird like in the story of Tico."

The children's reflections about their writing revealed the kinds of connections they made as they moved from reading literature to writing it. The teacher encouraged the children to draw from their own lives and their literary experiences to create original stories. Her goal was to help them develop an awareness of the fact that what an author composes is like a tapestry woven of many strands drawn from her or his literary history, inner life, personal experience, and imagination. Like Tico, each writer is unique, bringing to the page his or her "own memories, and invisible golden dreams" (Lionni, 1964, unpaged).

Assessment

Assessing the quality of children's involvement and understanding as readers, writers, and thinkers is an ongoing process throughout the cumulative experiences that make up the thematic literary unit. The teacher monitors the children's participation in the group sessions, their contributions to literary discussions, their independent reading, their journal entries, their written projects, and their use of other forms of creative expression to respond to literature. The teacher also makes note of a child's willingness to go beyond the limits of a specific assignment to engage in inquiry and further reading, writing, and/or creative expression. Because assessment is an ongoing process, the teacher can identify areas of weakness that need attention and offer new challenges to those who are ready for them. Objectives that were developed to guide the planning of the Wishes and Dreams unit were also used as criteria for the assessment process. The portfolio, a collection of representative samples of a given child's work, provided a useful vehicle for recording his or her involvement and growth over the course of the unit. When teacher and child examined the contents of the portfolio together, they could identify areas of strength and growth, as well as gaps in understandings or strategies that needed to be developed or reinforced. Together, they could develop plans to build on strengths and to address learning needs. In the course of the ongoing observation and evaluation of each child throughout the literary unit, and in the context of these private discussions about a child's portfolio, the teacher looked for signs that the students enjoyed the literary experiences in this unit. This was the first objective formulated for the Wishes and Dreams unit!

Concluding Comments

In the context of the thematic unit described in this chapter, a teacher and her students explored the world of literature together, collaboratively constructing meanings and building understandings and insights in the course of their literary journey. The children learned to respond to each new story in light of previously read literary texts and to use intertextual links with those texts to generate meaning and to study the craft of storytellers, authors, and artists. As engaged readers and writers, these children established an interpretive community in which they worked together to generate meaning as they talked about stories they read and stories they wrote. As they shared their experiences as readers and writers, they learned *from* each other and *about* each other.

In the course of this literary journey, the children were introduced to literature that stretched their minds and imaginations and touched their hearts, and they were challenged to become actively involved in the study of literature. During this cumulative experience, the children developed an awareness of some of the extraordinary interconnections between the world's many stories, both past and present. According to Jane Yolen (2000): "Stories lean on stories, art on art. This familiarity with the treasure-house of ancient story is necessary for any true appreciation of today's literature" (p. 15). Through literary discussions and independent reading and writing, the children who explored the wish and dream tales in the thematic literary unit described in this chapter discovered for themselves the validity of Yolen's words.

Children's Books Cited and Other Books Selected for the Wishes and Dreams Unit

Nonfiction

Brenner, Barbara. (1999). *The Boy Who Loved to Draw: Benjamin West*. Illustrated by Olivier Dunrea. Boston: Houghton Mifflin.

Demi, author and illustrator. (1999). *Kites: Magic Wishes That Fly Up to the Sky*. New York: Crown.

Knudson, R. Rozanne. (1985). *Babe Didrikson, Athlete of the Century*. Illustrated by Ted Lewin. New York: Viking Kestrel. [Early chapter book.]

Krull, Kathleen. (1996). *Wilma Unlimited: How Wilma Rudolph Became the World's Fastest Woman*. Illustrated by David Diaz. San Diego: Harcourt Brace.

Marzollo, Jean. (1993). *Happy Birthday, Martin Luther King*. Illustrated by J. Brian Pinkney. New York: Scholastic.

Miller, William. (1994). *Zora Hurston and the Chinaberry Tree*. Illustrated by Cornelius Van Wright and Ying-Hwa Hu. New York: Lee & Low Books.

Rosenthal, Bert. (1986). *Lynette Woodard: The First Female Globetrotter*. Chicago: Children's Press.

Sutcliffe, Jane. (2000). *Babe Didrikson Zaharias: All-Around Athlete*. Minneapolis: Carolrhoda Books. [For beginning readers.]

Wakeman, Nancy. (2000). *Babe Didrikson Zaharias: Driven to Win*. Minneapolis, MN: Lerner Publications.

Woods, Geraldine. (1987). *Jim Henson: From Puppets to Muppets*. Minneapolis: Dillon Press.

Poetry

Adoff, Arnold. (1989). *Chocolate Dreams: Poems*. Illustrated by Turi MacCombie. New York: Lothrop, Lee & Shepard.

Farjeon, Eleanor. (1992). "There Isn't Time." In *Inner Chimes: Poems on Poetry* (p. 3), selected by Bobbye S. Goldstein and illustrated by Jane Breskin Zalben. Honesdale, PA: Boyds Mills Press.

Florian, Douglas. (1994). "Delicious Wishes." In Douglas Florian, *Bing Bang Boing: Poems and Drawings* (p. 52). San Diego: Harcourt Brace.

Florian, Douglas. (1994). "Fish Wish." In Douglas Florian, *Bing Bang Boing: Poems and Drawings* (p. 69). San Diego: Harcourt Brace.

Glaser, Isabel Joshlin, selector. (1995). *Dreams of Glory: Poems Starring Girls*. Illustrated by Pat Lowery Collins. New York: Atheneum.

Hoberman, Mary Ann. (1998). "Wishes." In Mary Ann Hoberman, *The Llama Who Had No Pajama: 100 Favorite Poems* (p. 12), illustrated by Betty Fraser. San Diego: Harcourt Brace.

Hughes, Langston. (1988). "Dream Variation." In *Tomie dePaola's Book of Poems* (p. 87). New York: Putnam.

Kennedy, X. J. (1988). "The Forgetful Wishing Well." In *Tomie dePaola's Book of Poems* (p. 56). New York: Putnam.

Moore, Lilian. (1992). "Poets Go Wishing." In *Inner Chimes: Poems on Poetry* (p. 6), selected by Bobbye S. Goldstein and illustrated by Jane Breskin Zalben. Honesdale, PA: Boyds Mills Press.

Traditional and Modern Tales

Adoff, Arnold. (1988). *Flamboyan*. Illustrated by Karen Barbour. San Diego: Harcourt Brace Jovanovich.

Aiken, Joan. (1978). "Bridget's Hat." In *Tale of a One-Way Street and Other Stories* (pp. 41–56). Illustrated by Jan Pienkowski. Harmondsworth, Middlesex, England: Puffin Books.

Aiken, Joan. (1987). *The Moon's Revenge*. Illustrated by Alan Lee. New York: Knopf.

Anderson, Joy. (1986). *Juma and the Magic Jinn*. Illustrated by Charles Mikolaycak. New York: Lothrop, Lee & Shepard.

Avi. (2001). *The Secret School*. San Diego: Harcourt. [Chapter book.]

Bang, Molly, adapter. (1981). *Tye May and the Magic Brush*. New York: Greenwillow. [Adapted for beginning readers from an old Chinese tale.]

Bernatová, Eva. (1990). *The Wonder Shoes*. Illustrated by Fiona Moodie. New York: Farrar, Straus & Giroux.

Brenner, Barbara. (1992). *Rosa & Marco and the Three Wishes*. Illustrated by Megan Halsey. New York: Bradbury Press. [For beginning readers.]

Brett, Jan. (1981). *Fritz and the Beautiful Horses*. Boston: Houghton Mifflin.

Brittain, Bill. (1983). *The Wish Giver: Three Tales of Coven Tree*. Illustrated by Andrew Glass. New York: Harper & Row. [Early chapter book.]

Bruchac, Joseph, reteller. (1995). *Gluskabe and the Four Wishes*. Illustrated by Christine Nyburg Shrader. New York: Cobblehill/Dutton. [An Abenaki tale.]

Buehner, Caralyn. (1996). *Fanny's Dream*. Illustrated by Mark Buehner. New York: Dial.

Chapman, Carol. (1977). *Barney Bipple's Magic Dandelions*. Illustrated by Steven Kellogg. New York: Dutton.

Clifton, Lucille. (1992). *Three Wishes*. Illustrated by Michael Hays. New York: Delacorte Press.

Coursen, Valerie. (1997). *Mordant's Wish*. New York: Holt.

Craft, Charlotte, reteller. (1999). *King Midas and the Golden Touch*. Illustrated by Kinuko Craft. New York: Morrow.

Crew, Gary. (1997). *Bright Star*. Illustrated by Anne Spudvilas. Brooklyn: Kane/Miller Book Publishers.

Crisp, Marty. (2000). *My Dog, Cat*. Illustrated by True Kelley. New York: Holiday House. [Early chapter book.]

Demi, reteller. (1980). *Liang and the Magic Paintbrush*. New York: Holt, Rinehart, and Winston. [An old Chinese tale.]

Demi, adapter and illustrator. (1995). *The Magic Gold Fish: A Russian Folktale*. Adapted from Louis Zelikoff's translation of "The Tale of the Fisherman and the Little Fish" by Alexander Pushkin. New York: Holt.

Demi, adapter and illustrator. (2002). *King Midas: The Golden Touch*. New York: McElderry.

Doherty, Berlie. (1995). *The Magic Bicycle*. Illustrated by Christian Birmingham. New York: Crown Pub.

Egan, Tim. (1997). *Burnt Toast on Davenport Street*. Boston: Houghton Mifflin.

Elkin, Benjamin. (1960). *The King's Wish and Other Stories*. Illustrated by Leonard Shortall. New York: Beginner Books (distributed by Random House).

Fowler, Susi Gregg. (2000). *Albertina, the Animals, and Me*. Illustrated by Jim Fowler. New York: Greenwillow. [Early chapter book.]

Galdone, Paul, illustrator. (1961). *The Three Wishes*. New York: McGraw-Hill. [This retelling is from *More English Fairy Tales* (1894, Putnam), edited by Joseph Jacobs.]

Glass, Andrew. (1987). *Chickpea and the Talking Cow*. New York: Lothrop, Lee & Shepard.

Godden, Rumer, reteller. (1972). *The Old Woman Who Lived in a Vinegar Bottle*. Illustrated by Mairi Hedderwick. New York: Viking.

Grimm, Brothers. (1978). *The Fisherman and His Wife*. Translated by Elizabeth Shub. Illustrated by Monika Laimgruber. New York: Greenwillow.

Grimm, Brothers. (1985). *The Glass Mountain*. Adapted and illustrated by Nonny Hogrogian. New York: Knopf.

Grimm, Brothers. (1994). *The Seven Ravens*. Adapted by Laura Geringer with paintings by Edward Gazsi. New York: HarperCollins.

Guarnieri, Paolo. (1999). *A Boy Named Giotto*. Illustrated by Bimba Landmann. Translated by Jonathan Galassi. New York: Farrar Straus Giroux.

Hamberger, John. (1967). *The Wish*. New York: Norton.

Hautzig, Deborah, reteller. (1993). *Aladdin and the Magic Lamp*. Illustrated by Kathy Mitchell. New York: Random House. [For beginning readers.]

Hewitt, Kathryn, reteller and illustrator. (1987). *King Midas and the Golden Touch.* San Diego: Harcourt Brace Jovanovich. [Retold from the version by Nathaniel Hawthorne.]

Horn, Sandra Ann. (2000). *The Dandelion Wish.* Illustrated by Jason Cockcroft. New York: Dorling Kindersley.

Howe, James. (1987). *I Wish I Were a Butterfly.* Illustrated by Ed Young. San Diego: Harcourt Brace Jovanovich.

Hutchins, H. J. (1988). *The Three and Many Wishes of Jason Reid.* Illustrated by Julie Tennent. New York: Viking. [Early chapter book.]

Isadora, Rachel. (1993). *Lili at Ballet.* New York: Putnam's.

Jeschke, Susan. (1980). *Perfect the Pig.* New York: Holt, Rinehart, and Winston.

Kimmel, Eric, reteller. (1992). *The Tale of Aladdin and the Wonderful Lamp: A Story from the Arabian Nights.* Illustrated by Ju-Hong Chen. New York: Holiday House.

Krensky, Stephen. (2000). *The Youngest Fairy Godmother Ever.* Illustrated by Diana Bluthenthal. New York: Simon & Schuster.

Lewis, J. Patrick, reteller. (1999). *At the Wish of the Fish: An Adaptation of a Russian Folktale.* Illustrated by Katya Krenina. New York: Atheneum.

Lionni, Leo. (1964). *Tico and the Golden Wings.* New York: Pantheon.

Lionni, Leo. (1969). *Alexander and the Wind-Up Mouse.* New York: Pantheon.

Louie, Ai-Ling, reteller. (1982). *Yeh-Shen: A Cinderella Story from China.* Illustrated by Ed Young. New York: Philomel.

Lyon, George Ella. (1998). *A Sign.* Illustrated by Chris K. Soentpict. New York: Orchard.

MacDonald, Margaret Read, reteller. (1995). *The Old Woman Who Lived in a Vinegar Bottle.* Illustrated by Nancy Dunaway. Little Rock, AR: August House. [British fairy tale.]

Mayer, Marianna, reteller. (1990). *The Spirit of the Blue Light.* Illustrated by László Gál. New York: Macmillan. [German fairy tale.]

McClintock, Barbara, author and illustrator. (2001). *Molly and the Magic Wishbone.* New York: Farrar, Straus and Giroux.

McCully, Emily Arnold. (1992). *Mirette on the High Wire.* New York: Putnam's.

Mollel, Tololwa M. (1995). *Big Boy.* Illustrated by Earl B. Lewis. New York: Clarion Books.

Myers, Bernice. (1985). *Sydney Rella and the Glass Sneaker.* New York: Macmillan. [For beginning readers.]

O'Connor, Jane. (1996). *The Bad-Luck Penny.* Illustrated by Horatio Elena. New York: Grosset & Dunlap.

Orr, Wendy. (2000). *Ark in the Park.* Illustrated by Kerry Millard. New York: Henry Holt. [Early chapter book.]

Pastuchiv, Olga. (1997). *Minas and the Fish.* Boston: Houghton Mifflin.

Pfeffer, Susan Beth. (1996). *The Trouble with Wishes.* Illustrated by Jennifer Plecas. New York: Henry Holt. [Early chapter book.]

Pinkney, Andrea Davis. (1997). *Solo Girl.* Illustrated by Nneka Bennett. New York: Hyperion Books. [Early chapter book.]

Pinkney, Brian. (1997). *The Adventures of Sparrowboy.* New York: Simon & Schuster.

Polacco, Patricia. (1991). *Appelemando's Dreams.* New York: Philomel.

Polacco, Patricia. (1999). *Luba and the Wren.* New York: Philomel. [Russian variant of "The Fisherman and His Wife."]

Pryor, Bonnie. (1996). *The Dream Jar.* Illustrated by Mark Graham. New York: Morrow Jr. Books.

Pullman, Philip. (2000). *I Was a Rat!* Illustrated by Kevin Hawkes. New York: Knopf. [Chapter book.]

Quayle, Eric, compiler. (1989). "The Old Man Who Made Dead Trees Bloom." In *The Shining Princess and Other Japanese Legends* (pp. 69–76). Illustrated by Michael Foreman. New York: Arcade.

Ringgold, Faith. (1991). *Tar Beach.* New York: Crown Publishers.

Roth, Roger. (1993). *The Sign Painter's Dream.* New York: Crown Publishers.

Rylant, Cynthia. (1992). *An Angel for Solomon Singer.* Paintings by Peter Catalanotto. New York: Orchard Books.

Sachar, Louis. (2000). *A Magic Crystal?* Marvin Redpost series. New York: Random House. [Early chapter book.]

Sheldon, Dyan. (1997). *Unicorn Dreams.* Illustrated by Neil Reed. New York: Dial Books.

Singer, Isaac B., reteller. (1975). *A Tale of Three Wishes.* Illustrated by Irene Lieblich. New York: Farrar, Straus, and Giroux. [An old Jewish folktale.]

Speed, Toby. (1997). *Whoosh! Went the Wish.* Illustrated by Barry Root. New York: Putnam's.

Steig, William. (1969). *Sylvester and the Magic Pebble.* New York: Prentice-Hall.

Steptoe, John, reteller. (1984). *The Story of Jumping Mouse: A Native American Legend.* New York: Lothrop, Lee & Shepard Books.

Stewig, John Warren, reteller. (1999). *King Midas: A Golden Tale.* Illustrated by Omar Rayyan. New York: Holiday House.

Tan, Amy. (1992). *Moon Lady.* Illustrated by Gretchen Shields. New York: Macmillan.

Turkle, Brinton. (1981). *Do Not Open.* New York: Dutton.

Ward, Helen. (2001). *The Tin Forest.* Illustrated by Wayne Anderson. New York: Dutton.

Wells, Rosemary, adapter. (1998). *The Fisherman and His Wife.* Illustrated by Eleanor Hubbard. New York: Dial. [A new version of an old German tale.]

Wetterer, Margaret K. (1991). *The Boy Who Knew the Language of the Birds.* Illustrated by Beth Wright. Minneapolis: Carolrhoda. [An Irish fairy tale.]

Wildsmith, Brian. (1988). *Carousel.* New York: Knopf.

Williams, Jay. (1980). *One Big Wish.* Illustrated by John O'Brien. New York: Macmillan.

Williams, Karen. (1998). *Painted Dreams.* Illustrated by Catherine Stock. New York: Lothrop, Lee & Shepard.

Wilson, Barbara Ker, reteller. (1993). *Wishbones: A Folk Tale from China.* Illustrated by Meilo So. New York: Bradbury Press.

Wojciechowski, Susan. (1997). *Beany (Not Beanhead) and the Magic Crystal.* Illustrated by Susanna Natti. Cambridge, MA: Candlewick Press. [Early chapter book.]

Wolkstein, Diane, reteller. (1983). *The Magic Wings: A Tale from China.* Illustrated by Robert Andrew Parker. New York: Dutton.

Wood, Audrey. (2000). *Jubal's Wish.* Illustrated by Don Wood. New York: Blue Sky Press.

Yolen, Jane. (1968). *Greyling: A Picture Story from the Islands of Shetland.* Illustrated by William Stobbs. Cleveland, OH: World Publishing.

Yolen, Jane. (1977). "The Wind Cap." In *The Hundredth Dove and Other Tales* (pp. 19–27). New York: Crowell.

Yolen, Jane. (1981). *Sleeping Ugly.* New York: Coward-McCann. [For beginning readers.]

Yolen, Jane. (1991). *Greyling.* Illustrated by David Ray. New York: Philomel.

Zemach, Margot, reteller. (1986). *The Three Wishes: An Old Story.* New York: Farrar, Straus, and Giroux.

Appendix A: Resources for Teachers

Children's Literature in the Classroom

Benedict, Susan, & Carlisle, Lenore. (Eds.). (1992). *Beyond words: Picture books for older readers and writers.* Portsmouth, NH: Heinemann.

Blatt, Gloria T. (Ed.). (1993). *Once upon a folktale: Capturing the folklore process with children.* New York: Teachers College Press.

Bromley, Karen D'Angelo. (1996). *Webbing with literature: Creating story maps with children's books* (2nd ed.). Boston, MA: Allyn & Bacon.

Cullinan, B. E., Scala, M. C., & Schroder, V. C., with Lovett, A. K. (1995). *Three voices: An invitation to poetry across the curriculum.* York, ME: Stenhouse.

Egoff, Sheila A., Stubbs, G., Ashley, R., & Sutton, W. (Eds.). (1996). *Only connect: Readings on children's literature* (3rd ed.). New York: Oxford University Press.

Farrell, Edmund, & Squire, James. (1990). *Transactions with literature: A fifty-year perspective.* Urbana, IL: National Council of Teachers of English.

Fletcher, Ralph, & Portalupi, Joann. (1998). *Craft lessons: Teaching writing K–8.* York, ME: Stenhouse.

Gambrell, Linda, & Almasi, Janice. (Eds.). (1996). *Lively discussions! Fostering engaged reading.* Newark, DE: International Reading Association.

Hancock, Marjorie R. (2000). *A celebration of literature and response: Children, books, and teachers in K–8 classrooms.* Upper Saddle River, NJ: Merrill.

Hansen, Jane. (1987). *When writers read.* Portsmouth, NH: Heinemann.

Harris, Violet J. (Ed.). (1997). *Using multiethnic literature in the K–8 classroom.* Norwood, MA: Christopher-Gordon.

Harwayne, Shelley. (1992). *Lasting impressions: Weaving literature in the writing workshop.* Portsmouth, NH: Heinemann.

Hickman, Janet, & Cullinan, Bernice. (Eds.). (1989). *Children's literature in the classroom: Weaving Charlotte's web.* Needham Heights, MA: Christopher-Gordon.

Holdaway, Don. (1979). *The foundations of literacy.* Sydney, Australia: Ashton Scholastic.

Holland, Kathleen E., Hungerford, Rachael A., & Ernst, Shirley B. (Eds.) (1993). *Journeying: Children responding to literature.* Portsmouth, NH: Heinemann.

Hopkins, L. B. (1998). *Pass the poetry, please!* New York: HarperCollins.

Huck, Charlotte S., Hepler, Susan, Hickman, Janet, & Barbara Kiefer. (2001). *Children's literature in the elementary school* (7th ed.). Dubuque, IA: McGraw-Hill.

Jenkins, Carol Brennan. (1999). *The allure of authors: Author studies in the elementary classroom*. Portsmouth, NH: Heinemann.

Kiefer, Barbara Z. (1995). *The potential of picturebooks: From visual literacy to aesthetic understanding*. Englewood Cliffs, NJ: Merrill.

Koch, K. (1999). *Wishes, lies, and dreams: Teaching children to write poetry*. New York: HarperPerennial.

Langer, Judith A. (Ed.). (1992). *Literature instruction: A focus on student response*. Urbana, IL: National Council of Teachers of English.

Langer, Judith A. (1995). *Envisioning literature: Literary understanding and literature instruction*. New York: Teachers College Press.

Lukens, Rebecca. (1999). *A critical handbook of children's literature* (6th ed.). New York: Longman.

Marcus, Leonard S. (Ed.). (2000). *Author talk*. New York: Simon & Schuster. [Fifteen short conversations with well-known children's authors.]

Moss, Joy F. (1996). *Teaching literature in the elementary school: A thematic approach*. Norwood, MA: Christopher-Gordon.

Moss, Joy F. (2000). *Teaching literature in the middle grades: A thematic approach* (2nd ed.). Norwood, MA: Christopher-Gordon.

Norton, Donna E., with Norton, Sandra E. (1999). *Through the eyes of the child: An introduction to children's literature* (5th ed.). Upper Saddle River, NJ: Merrill/Prentice-Hall.

Paterson, K. (1981). *Gates of excellence: On reading and writing books for children*. New York: Elsevier/Nelson Books.

Paterson, K. (1989). *The spying heart: More thoughts on reading and writing books for children*. New York: Lodestar.

Paterson, K. (2001). *The invisible child: On reading and writing books for children*. New York: Dutton.

Peterson, R., & Eeds, M. (1990). *Grand conversations: Literature groups in action*. New York: Scholastic.

Rosenblatt, Louise. (1938/76). *Literature as exploration*. New York: Noble and Noble.

Rosenblatt, Louise. (1978). *The reader, the text, and the poem*. Carbondale, IL: Southern Illinois University Press.

Roser, Nancy L., & Martinez, Miriam G. (Eds.). (1995). *Book talk and beyond: Children and teachers respond to literature*. Newark, DE: International Reading Association.

Sebesta, Sam. (2001, Summer). "What do teachers need to know about children's literature?" *New Advocate, 14*(3), 241–249.

Short, K. G. (Ed.). (1995). *Research and professional resources in children's literature: Piecing a patchwork quilt.* Newark, DE: International Reading Association.

Stoodt-Hill, Barbara D., & Amspaugh-Corson, Linda B. (2001). *Children's literature: Discovery for a lifetime* (2nd ed.). Upper Saddle River, NJ: Prentice-Hall.

Tiedt, Iris McClellan. (2000). *Teaching with picture books in the middle school.* Newark, DE: International Reading Association.

Tomlinson, Carl, & Lynch-Brown, Carol. (2002). *Essentials of children's literature* (4th ed.). Boston: Allyn and Bacon.

Tunnell, M. O., & Jacobs, J. S. (2000). *Children's literature, briefly* (2nd ed.). Upper Saddle River, NJ: Merrill.

Whitin, Phyllis. (1996). *Sketching stories, stretching minds: Responding visually to literature.* Portsmouth, NH: Heinemann.

Yolen, Jane. (2000). *Touch magic: Fantasy, faerie, and folklore in the literature of childhood.* Little Rock, AR: August House.

Zipes, J. D. (2000). *Sticks and stones: The troublesome success of children's literature from Slovenly Peter to Harry Potter.* New York: Routledge.

Book Selection Aids

A to Zoo: Subject Access to Children's Picture Books (6th ed.). (1993). Compiled by Carolyn W. Lima and John A. Lima. New Providence, NJ: Bowker.

Adventuring with Books: A Booklist for Pre-K–Grade 6 (12th ed.). (2000). Edited by Kathryn Mitchell Pierce. Urbana, IL: National Council of Teachers of English.

The Bulletin of the Center for Children's Books. Urbana, IL: University of Illinois Press. [Eleven issues published each year.]

Celebrating Children's Choices: 25 Years of Children's Favorite Books. (2000). Arden DeVries Post. Newark, DE: International Reading Association.

The Horn Book Guide to Children's and Young Adult Books. Boston: MA: Horn Book. [Published twice a year.]

Kaleidoscope: A Multicultural Booklist for Grades K–8 (3rd ed.). (2001). Edited by Junko Yokota. Urbana, IL: National Council of Teachers of English.

Through Indian Eyes: The Native Experience in Books for Children. Beverly Slapin and Doris Seale. Los Angeles: American Indian Studies Center.

Journals and Periodicals

Book Links. American Library Association, 50 E. Huron St., Chicago, IL 60611. [Six times a year.]

Children's Literature in Education. Agathon Press, 233 Spring St., New York, NY 10013. [Quarterly.]

Horn Book Magazine. Horn Book, Inc., 56 Roland St., Suite 200, Boston, MA 02129. [Bimonthly.]

Language Arts. National Council of Teachers of English, 1111 W. Kenyon Rd., Urbana, IL 61801-1096. [Bimonthly.]

The Lion and the Unicorn: A Critical Journal of Children's Literature. Johns Hopkins University Press, 2715 N. Charles St., Baltimore, MD 21218. [Annual.]

Marvels and Tales: Journal of Fairy-Tale Studies. Wayne State University Press, 4809 Woodward Avenue, Detroit, MI 48201.

The New Advocate. Christopher-Gordon, 1502 Providence Hwy., Suite 12, Norwood, MA 02062. [Quarterly.]

The Reading Teacher. International Reading Association, 800 Barksdale Road, PO Box 8139, Newark, DE 19714.

School Library Journal. PO Box 57559, Boulder, CO 80322.

Theory into Practice. Ohio State University, Arps Hall, 1945 N. High St., Columbus, OH 43210.

Voices from the Middle. National Council of Teachers of English. 1111 W. Kenyon Rd., Urbana, IL 61801-1096. [Quarterly.]

THE WEB: Wonderfully Exciting Books. Ohio State University, The Reading Center, 200 Ramseyer Hall, Columbus, OH 43210. [Three times a year.]

Web Sites

The Association for Library Services to Children: http://www.ala.org/alsc/

The Children's Book Council: http://www.cbcbooks.org/

The Cooperative Children's Book Center (CCBC): http://www.soemadison.wisc.edu/ccbc/

The International Reading Association: http://www.reading.org/

The National Council of Teachers of English: http://www.ncte.org/

Appendix B: Children's Literature by Category

Picture Storybooks

Adoff, Arnold. (1988). *Flamboyan*. Illustrated by Karen Barbour. San Diego: Harcourt Brace Jovanovich.

Alexander, Lloyd. (1971). *The King's Fountain*. Illustrated by Ezra Jack Keats. New York: Dutton.

Anderson, Joy. (1986). *Juma and the Magic Jinn*. Illustrated by Charles Mikolaycak. New York: Lothrop, Lee & Shepard.

Aylesworth, Jim. (1999). *The Full Belly Bowl*. Illustrated by Wendy Anderson Halperin. New York: Atheneum.

Barracca, Debra, & Barracca, Sal. (1990). *The Adventures of Taxi Dog*. Illustrated by Mark Buehner. New York: Dial.

Berenzy, Alix. (1989). *A Frog Prince*. New York: Henry Holt.

Bernatová, Eva. (1990). *The Wonder Shoes*. Illustrated by Fiona Moodie. New York: Farrar, Straus & Giroux.

Blake, Robert J. (1997). *Akiak: A Tale from the Iditarod*. New York: Philomel.

Brett, Jan. (1981). *Fritz and the Beautiful Horses*. Boston: Houghton Mifflin.

Buehner, Caralyn. (1996). *Fanny's Dream*. Illustrated by Mark Buehner. New York: Dial.

Bunting, Eve. (1991). *Fly Away Home*. Illustrated by Ronald Himler. New York: Clarion.

Bushey, Jeanne. (1994). *A Sled Dog for Moshi*. Illustrated by Germaine Arnaktauyok. New York: Hyperion.

Carrick, Carol. (1974). *Lost in the Storm*. Illustrated by Donald Carrick. New York: Clarion.

Chapman, Carol. (1977). *Barney Bipple's Magic Dandelions*. Illustrated by Steven Kellogg. New York: Dutton.

Christelow, Eileen. (1992). *Gertrude, the Bulldog Detective*. New York: Clarion.

Clifton, Lucille. (1992). *Three Wishes*. Illustrated by Michael Hays. New York: Delacorte.

Coursen, Valerie. (1997). *Mordant's Wish*. New York: Holt.

Crew, Gary. (1997). *Bright Star*. Illustrated by Anne Spudvilas. Brooklyn: Kane/Miller Book Publishers.

Doherty, Berlie. (1995). *The Magic Bicycle*. Illustrated by Christian Birmingham. New York: Crown Pub.

Egan, Tim. (1997). *Burnt Toast on Davenport Street.* Boston: Houghton Mifflin.

Ezra, Mark. (1996). *The Hungry Otter.* Illustrated by Gavin Rowe. New York: Crocodile Books.

Franklin, Kristine. (1996). *The Wolfhound.* Illustrated by Kris Waldherr. New York: Lothrop, Lee & Shepard.

Glass, Andrew. (1987). *Chickpea and the Talking Cow.* New York: Lothrop Lee & Shepard.

Guarnieri, Paolo. (1999). *A Boy Named Giotto.* Illustrated by Bimba Landmann. Translated by Jonathan Galassi. New York: Farrar Straus Giroux.

Hamberger, John. (1967). *The Wish.* New York: Norton.

Heide, Florence Parry, & Gilliland, Judith Heide. (1992). *Sami and the Time of the Troubles.* Illustrated by Ted Lewin. New York: Clarion.

Horn, Sandra Ann. (2000). *The Dandelion Wish.* Illustrated by Jason Cockcroft. New York: Dorling Kindersley.

Hort, Lenny, reteller. (1987). *The Boy Who Held Back the Sea.* Illustrated by Thomas Locker. New York: Dial.

Howard, Elizabeth Fitzgerald. (2000). *Virgie Goes to School with Us Boys.* Illustrated by E. B. Lewis. New York: Simon & Schuster.

Howe, James. (1987). *I Wish I Were a Butterfly.* Illustrated by Ed Young. San Diego: Harcourt Brace Jovanovich.

Innocenti, Roberto, & Gallaz, Christophe. (1985). *Rose Blanche.* Translated by Martha Coventry & Richard Graglia. Mankato, MN: Creative Education.

Isadora, Rachel. (1993). *Lili at Ballet.* New York: Putnam's.

Jeschke, Susan. (1980). *Perfect the Pig.* New York: Holt, Rinehart and Winston.

Jiménez, Francisco. (1998). *La Mariposa.* Boston: Houghton Mifflin.

Jones, Carol. (1997). *The Lion and the Mouse.* Boston: Houghton Mifflin.

Kellogg, Steven. (1979). *Pinkerton, Behave!* New York: Dial.

Korschunow, Irina. (1984). *The Foundling Fox.* Illustrated by Reinhard Michl. Translated by James Skofield. New York: Harper & Row.

Krensky, Stephen. (2000). *The Youngest Fairy Godmother Ever.* Illustrated by Diana Bluthenthal. New York: Simon & Schuster.

Lionni, Leo. (1964). *Tico and the Golden Wings.* New York: Pantheon.

Lionni, Leo. (1967). *Frederick.* New York: Pantheon.

Lionni, Leo. (1969). *Alexander and the Wind-Up Mouse.* New York: Pantheon.

Lyon, George Ella. (1998). *A Sign.* Illustrated by Chris K. Soentpict. New York: Orchard.

McCully, Emily Arnold. (1992). *Mirette on the High Wire.* New York: Putnam's.

Meddaugh, Susan. (1992). *Martha Speaks.* Boston: Houghton Mifflin.

Mochizuki, Ken. (1997). *Passage to Freedom: The Sugihara Story.* Illustrated by Dom Lee. New York: Lee & Low.

Mollel, Tololwa M. (1995). *Big Boy.* Illustrated by Earl B. Lewis. New York: Clarion Books.

Myers, Christopher A. (2000). *Wings.* New York: Scholastic Press.

Oppenheim, Shulamith Levey. (1992). *The Lily Cupboard.* Illustrated by Ronald Himler. New York: HarperCollins.

Park, Frances, and Park, Ginger. (2000). *The Royal Bee.* Illustrated by Christopher Zhong-Yuan Zhang. Honesdale, PA: Boyds Mills Press.

Pastuchiv, Olga. (1997). *Minas and the Fish.* Boston: Houghton Mifflin.

Paulsen, Gary. (1993). *Dogteam.* Illustrated by Ruth Wright Paulsen. New York: Delacorte Press. [Prose poem.]

Peet, Bill. (1972). *The Ant and the Elephant.* Boston: Houghton Mifflin.

Pinkney, Brian. (1997). *The Adventures of Sparrowboy.* New York: Simon & Schuster.

Polacco, Patricia. (1991). *Appelemando's Dreams.* New York: Philomel.

Polacco, Patricia. (1998). *Thank You, Mr. Falker.* New York: Philomel.

Polacco, Patricia. (2000). *The Butterfly.* New York: Philomel.

Pryor, Bonnie. (1996). *The Dream Jar.* Illustrated by Mark Graham. New York: Morrow Jr. Books.

Ringgold, Faith. (1991). *Tar Beach.* New York: Crown Publishers.

Roth, Roger. (1993). *The Sign Painter's Dream.* New York: Crown Publishers.

Rylant, Cynthia. (1992). *An Angel for Solomon Singer.* Paintings by Peter Catalanotto. New York: Orchard Books.

Scieszka, Jon. (1989). *The True Story of the Three Little Pigs by A. Wolf.* Illustrated by Lane Smith. New York: Viking Kestrel.

Sendak, Maurice. (1963). *Where the Wild Things Are.* New York: Harper & Row.

Seymour, Tres. (1993). *Pole Dog.* Illustrated by David Soman. New York: Orchard.

Sheldon, Dyan. (1997). *Unicorn Dreams.* Illustrated by Neil Reed. New York: Dial Books.

Slobodkin, Louis. (1955). *The Amiable Giant.* New York: Vanguard Press.

Snyder, Zilpha Keatley. (1985). *The Changing Maze.* Illustrated by Charles Mikolaycak. New York: Macmillan.

Speed, Toby. (1997). *Whoosh! Went the Wish.* Illustrated by Barry Root. New York: Putnam's.

Stanley, Diane. (1997). *Rumpelstiltskin's Daughter.* New York: Morrow.

Steig, William. (1969). *Sylvester and the Magic Pebble.* New York: Prentice-Hall.

Stolz, Mary. (1991). *Deputy Shep.* Illustrated by Pamela Johnson. New York: HarperCollins.

Tan, Amy. (1992). *Moon Lady.* Illustrated by Gretchen Shields. New York: Macmillan.

Thompson, Colin. (2000). *Unknown.* Illustrated by Anna Pignatrao. New York: Walker.

Turkle, Brinton. (1976). *Deep in the Forest.* New York: Dutton.

Turkle, Brinton. (1981). *Do Not Open.* New York: Dutton.

Van Allsburg, Chris. (1983). *The Wreck of the Zephyr.* Boston: Houghton Mifflin.

Van Allsburg, Chris. (1991). *The Wretched Stone.* Boston: Houghton Mifflin.

Vincent, Gabrielle. (1999). *a day, a dog.* Asheville, NC: Front Street. [Wordless book.]

Ward, Helen. (2001). *The Tin Forest.* Illustrated by Wayne Anderson. New York: Dutton.

Wildsmith, Brian. (1988). *Carousel.* New York: Knopf.

Williams, Jay. (1980). *One Big Wish.* Illustrated by John O'Brien. New York: Macmillan.

Williams, Karen. (1998). *Painted Dreams.* Illustrated by Catherine Stock. New York: Lothrop, Lee & Shepard.

Wood, Audrey. (2000). *Jubal's Wish.* Illustrated by Don Wood. New York: Blue Sky Press.

Woodson, Jacqueline. (2001). *The Other Side.* Illustrated by Earl B. Lewis. New York: Putnam's.

Yashima, Taro. (1955). *Crow Boy.* New York: Viking.

Yolen, Jane. (1968). *Greyling: A Picture Story from the Islands of Shetland.* Illustrated by William Stobbs. Cleveland, OH: World Publishing.

Yolen, Jane. (1991). *Greyling.* Illustrated by David Ray. New York: Philomel.

Traditional Literature

Aesop. (1947). *Aesop's Fables.* Illustrated by Fritz Kredel. New York: Grosset and Dunlap.

Arnold, Katya, reteller and illustrator. (2000). *That Apple Is Mine!* Based on a story by Vladimir Suteev. New York: Holiday House.

Barber, Antonia, reteller. (1998). *Apollo & Daphne: Masterpieces of Greek Mythology.* [With paintings from the great art museums of the world.] Los Angeles: J. Paul Getty Museum.

Belpré, Pura, reteller. (1978). *The Rainbow-Colored Horse.* Illustrated by Antonio Martorell. New York: Frederick Warne.

Brett, Jan, reteller and illustrator. (1989). *Beauty and the Beast.* New York: Clarion Books.

Bruchac, Joseph, reteller. (1995). *Gluskabe and the Four Wishes.* Illustrated by Christine Nyburg Shrader. New York: Cobblehill/Dutton. [An Abenaki tale.]

Byrd, Robert. (1999). *Finn MacCoul and His Fearless Wife: A Giant of a Tale from Ireland.* New York: Dutton Children's Books.

Climo, Shirley, reteller. (1993). *The Korean Cinderella.* Illustrated by Ruth Heller. New York: HarperCollins.

Climo, Shirley, reteller. (1995). *Atalanta's Race: A Greek Myth.* Illustrated by Alexander Koshkin. New York: Clarion.

Coburn, Jewell Rinehart. (1998). *Angkat, the Cambodian Cinderella.* Illustrated by Eddie Flotte. Auburn, CA: Shen's Books.

Coolidge, Olivia. (1952). *The Trojan War.* Illustrated by Edouard Sandoz. Boston: Houghton Mifflin.

Craft, Charlotte, reteller. (1999). *King Midas and the Golden Touch.* Illustrated by Kinuko Craft. New York: Morrow.

Dasent, George Webbe, translator. (1991). *East o' the Sun and West o' the Moon.* Illustrated by Patrick James Lynch. Cambridge, MA: Candlewick Press. [A Norwegian fairy tale.]

D'Aulaire, Ingri, & D'Aulaire, Edgar Parin. (1962). *Book of Greek Myths.* New York: Doubleday.

Demi, reteller. (1980). *Liang and the Magic Paintbrush.* New York: Holt, Rinehart, and Winston. [An old Chinese tale.]

Demi, adapter and illustrator. (1995). *The Magic Gold Fish: A Russian Folktale.* Adapted from Louis Zelikoff's translation of "The Tale of the Fisherman and the Little Fish" by Alexander Pushkin. New York: Holt.

Demi, adapter and illustrator. (2002). *King Midas: The Golden Touch.* New York: McElderry.

DePaola, Tomie, reteller. (1981). *Fin M'Coul: The Giant of Knockmany Hill.* New York: Holiday House.

Fisher, Leonard Everett. (1988). *Theseus and the Minotaur.* New York: Holiday House.

Fisher, Leonard Everett. (1991). *Cyclops.* New York: Holiday House.

Galdone, Paul, illustrator. (1961). *The Three Wishes.* New York: McGraw-Hill. [This retelling is from *More English Fairy Tales* (1894, Putnam), edited by Joseph Jacobs.]

Godden, Rumer, reteller. (1972). *The Old Woman Who Lived in a Vinegar Bottle.* Illustrated by Mairi Hedderwick. New York: Viking.

Gregorowski, Christopher, reteller. (2000). *Fly, Eagle, Fly! An African Tale.* Foreword by Archbishop Desmond Tutu. Illustrated by Niki Daly. New York: McElderry Books.

Grimm, Brothers. (1978). *The Fisherman and His Wife.* Translated by Elizabeth Shub. Illustrated by Monika Laimgruber. New York: Greenwillow.

Grimm, Brothers. (1985). *The Glass Mountain.* Adapted and illustrated by Nonny Hogrogian. New York: Knopf.

Grimm, Brothers. (1994). *The Seven Ravens.* Adapted by Laura Geringer with paintings by Edward Gazsi. New York: HarperCollins.

Hamilton, Virginia. (2000). *The Girl Who Spun Gold.* Illustrated by Leo Dillon and Diane Dillon. New York: Blue Sky Press.

Hewitt, Kathryn, reteller and illustrator. (1987). *King Midas and the Golden Touch.* San Diego: Harcourt Brace Jovanovich. [Retold from the version by Nathaniel Hawthorne.]

Heyer, Marilee, reteller. (1986). *The Weaving of a Dream: A Chinese Folktale.* New York: Viking.

Hickox, Rebecca. (1998). *The Golden Sandal: A Middle Eastern Cinderella Story.* Illustrated by Will Hillenbrand. New York: Holiday House.

Hovey, Kate, reteller. (2000). *Arachne Speaks.* Illustrated by Blair Drawson. New York: McElderry.

Hutton, Warwick. (1992). *The Trojan Horse.* New York: Macmillan.

Jaffe, Nina. (1998). *The Way Meat Loves Salt: A Cinderella Tale from the Jewish Tradition.* Illustrated by Louise August. New York: Holt.

Kimmel, Eric, reteller. (1992). *The Tale of Aladdin and the Wonderful Lamp: A Story from the Arabian Nights.* Illustrated by Ju-Hong Chen. New York: Holiday House.

Kimmel, Eric, adapter. (1997). *Sirko and the Wolf: A Ukrainian Tale.* Illustrated by Rob Sauber. New York: Holiday House.

Lee, Jeanne M. (1995). *The Song of Mu Lan.* Arden, NC: Front Street.

Lewis, J. Patrick, reteller. (1999). *At the Wish of the Fish: An Adaptation of a Russian Folktale.* Illustrated by Katya Krenina. New York: Atheneum.

Louie, Ai-Ling, reteller. (1982). *Yeh-Shen: A Cinderella Story from China.* Illustrated by Ed Young. New York: Philomel.

MacDonald, Margaret Read, reteller. (1995). *The Old Woman Who Lived in a Vinegar Bottle.* Illustrated by Nancy Dunaway. Little Rock, AR: August House.

Manning-Sanders, Ruth. (1972). *A Book of Ogres and Trolls.* Illustrated by Robin Jacques. New York: Dutton.

Marsoli, Lisa Ann, adapter. (1998). *Disney's Mulan.* Illustrated by Judith Clarke. Burbank, CA: MouseWorks.

Martin, Rafe, reteller. (1998). *The Brave Little Parrot.* Illustrated by Susan Gaber. New York: Putnam.

Mayer, Marianna, reteller. (1990). *The Spirit of the Blue Light.* Illustrated by László Gál. New York: Macmillan.

Mayer, Marianna. (1998). *Pegasus*. Illustrated by Kinuko Craft. New York: Morrow.

McBratney, Sam. (1998). *Celtic Myths*. Illustrated by Stephen Player. New York: Peter Bedrick Books.

McCaughrean, Geraldine, reteller. (1998). *The Bronze Cauldron: Myths and Legends of the World*. Illustrated by Bee Willey. New York: McElderry Books.

McCaughrean, Geraldine, reteller. (1998). *Greek Gods and Goddesses*. Illustrated by Emma Chichester Clark. New York: McElderry Books.

Morley, Jacqueline. (1998). *Greek Myths*. Illustrated by Giovanni Caselli. New York: Peter Bedrick Books.

Newton, Patricia Montgomery, adapter. (1982). *The Five Sparrows: A Japanese Folktale*. New York: Atheneum.

Nones, Eric Jon, translator and illustrator. (1991). *The Canary Prince*. New York: Farrar, Straus, and Giroux.

Norman, Howard A., reteller. (1989). *How Glooskap Outwits the Ice Giants and Other Tales of the Maritime Indians*. Wood Engravings by Michael McCurdy. Boston: Little, Brown.

Oppenheim, Joanne, adapter. (1992). *One Gift Deserves Another*. Illustrated by Bo Zaunders. New York: Dutton.

Orgel, Doris, reteller. (2000). *The Lion and the Mouse and Other Aesop's Fables*. Illustrated by Bert Kitchen. New York: Dorling Kindersley.

Osborne, Mary Pope. (1996). *Favorite Norse Myths*. Illustrated by Troy Howell. New York: Scholastic.

Pastuchiv, Olga. (1997). *Minas and the Fish*. Boston: Houghton Mifflin.

Paxton, reteller. (1996). *The Ant and the Grasshopper: An Aesop's Fable*. Illustrated by Philip Webb. Glenview, IL: Celebration Press.

Philip, Neil, reteller. (1996). *Odin's Family: Myths of the Vikings*. Illustrated by Maryclare Foa. New York: Orchard Books.

Philip, Neil, reteller. (1997). *The Adventures of Odysseus*. Illustrated by Peter Malone. New York: Orchard Books.

Pinkney, Jerry, illustrator. (2000). "The Grasshopper and the Ants." In *Aesop's Fables* (pp. 12–13). New York: SeaStar Books.

Pitre, Felix, reteller. (1995). *Paco and the Witch*. New York: Lodestar.

Polacco, Patricia. (1999). *Luba and the Wren*. New York: Philomel. [Russian variant of "The Fisherman and His Wife."]

Poole, Amy Lowry, reteller and illustrator. (2000). *The Ant and the Grasshopper*. New York: Holiday House.

Quayle, Eric, compiler. (1989). "The Old Man Who Made Dead Trees Bloom." In *The Shining Princess and Other Japanese Legends* (pp. 69–76). Illustrated by Michael Foreman. New York: Arcade.

Sanderson, Ruth, reteller. (1995). *Papa Gatto: An Italian Fairy Tale.* Boston: Little Brown.

San Souci, Robert D., reteller. (1989). *The Talking Eggs: A Folktale from the American South.* Illustrated by Jerry Pinkney. New York: Dial.

San Souci, Robert D. (1998). *Cendrillon: A Caribbean Cinderella.* Illustrated by J. Brian Pinkney. New York: Simon & Schuster.

San Souci, Robert D., reteller. (1998). *Fa Mulan: The Story of a Woman Warrior.* Illustrated by Jean Tseng and Mou-Sien Tseng. New York: Hyperion.

Sierra, Judy. (1997). *The Mean Hyena: A Folktale from Malawi.* Illustrated by Michael Bryant. New York: Lodestar Books.

Singer, Isaac B., reteller. (1975). *A Tale of Three Wishes.* Illustrated by Irene Lieblich. New York: Farrar, Straus, and Giroux.

Steptoe, John, reteller. (1984). *The Story of Jumping Mouse: A Native American Legend.* New York: Lothrop, Lee & Shepard.

Steptoe, John, reteller. (1987). *Mufaro's Beautiful Daughters: An African Tale.* New York: Lothrop, Lee & Shepard.

Stewig, John W., reteller. (1995). *Princess Florecita and the Iron Shoes: A Spanish Fairy Tale.* Illustrated by Wendy Popp. New York: Knopf.

Stewig, John W., reteller. (1999). *King Midas.* Illustrated by Omar Rayyan. New York: Holiday House.

Sutcliff, Rosemary, reteller. (1996). *The Wanderings of Odysseus: The Story of the Odyssey.* Illustrated by Alan Lee. New York: Delacorte.

Tchana, Katrin. (2000). *The Serpent Slayer and Other Stories of Strong Women.* Illustrated by Trina Schart Hyman. Boston: Little, Brown.

Torre, Betty. (1990). *The Luminous Pearl: A Chinese Folktale.* Illustrated by Carol Inouye. New York: Orchard Books.

Waldherr, Kris, reteller and illustrator. (1995). *The Book of Goddesses.* Hillsboro, OR: Beyond Words Publishing.

Watts, Bernadette, reteller. (2000). *The Lion and the Mouse: An Aesop Fable.* New York: North-South Books.

Wells, Rosemary, adapter. (1998). *The Fisherman and His Wife.* Illustrated by Eleanor Hubbard. New York: Dial.

Wetterer, Margaret K. (1991). *The Boy Who Knew the Language of the Birds.* Illustrated by Beth Wright. Minneapolis: Carolrhoda.

Wilson, Barbara Ker, reteller. (1993). *Wishbones: A Folk Tale from China.* Illustrated by Meilo So. New York: Bradbury Press.

Wolkstein, Diane, reteller. (1983). *The Magic Wings: A Tale from China.* Illustrated by Robert Andrew Parker. New York: Dutton.

Yep, Laurence, reteller. (1997). *The Dragon Prince: A Chinese Beauty and the Beast Tale.* Illustrated by Kam Mak. New York: HarperCollins.

Yolen, Jane. (1991). *Wings.* Illustrated by Dennis Nolan. San Diego: Harcourt Brace Jovanovich.

Yolen, Jane. (1998). *Pegasus, the Flying Horse.* Illustrated by Ming Li. New York: Dutton.

Young, Ed, reteller and illustrator. (1979). *The Lion and the Mouse: An Aesop Fable.* Garden City, NY: Doubleday.

Young, Ed, translator and illustrator. (1989). *Lon Po Po: A Red-Riding Hood Story from China.* New York: Philomel.

Young, Ed, reteller and illustrator. (1994). *Little Plum.* New York: Philomel.

Zemach, Margot, reteller. (1986). *The Three Wishes: An Old Story.* New York: Farrar, Straus, and Giroux.

Modern Fantasy

Aiken, Joan. (1978). "Bridget's Hat." In *Tale of a One-Way Street and Other Stories* (pp. 41–56). Illustrated by Jan Pienkowski. Harmondsworth, Middlesex, England: Puffin Books.

Aiken, Joan. (1987). *The Moon's Revenge.* Illustrated by Alan Lee. New York: Knopf.

Helldorfer, Mary-Claire. (1991). *The Mapmaker's Daughter.* Illustrated by Jonathan Hunt. New York: Bradbury Press.

McClintock, Barbara, author and illustrator. (2001). *Molly and the Magic Wishbone.* New York: Farrar, Straus and Giroux.

Meddaugh, Susan. (1997). *Cinderella's Rat.* Boston: Houghton Mifflin.

Paterson, Katherine. (1992). *The King's Equal.* Illustrated by Vladimir Vasil'evich Vagin. New York: HarperCollins.

Pullman, Philip. (2000). *I Was a Rat!* Illustrated by Kevin Hawkes. New York: Knopf.

Thurber, James. (1944/1994). *The Great Quillow.* Illustrated by Steven Kellogg. San Diego: Harcourt Brace.

Yolen, Jane. (1980). "The Hundredth Dove." In Jane Yolen, *The Hundredth Dove and Other Tales.* Illustrated by David Palladini. New York: Schocken Books.

Books for Beginning Readers

Bang, Molly, adapter. (1981). *Tye May and the Magic Brush.* New York: Greenwillow.

Brenner, Barbara. (1992). *Rosa & Marco and the Three Wishes.* Illustrated by Megan Halsey. New York: Bradbury Press.

Elkin, Benjamin. (1960). *The King's Wish and Other Stories.* Illustrated by Leonard Shortall. New York: Beginner Books (distributed by Random House).

Hautzig, Deborah, reteller. (1993). *Aladdin and the Magic Lamp.* Illustrated by Kathy Mitchell. New York: Random House.

Herman, Gail. (1998). *The Lion and the Mouse.* Illustrated by Lisa McCue. New York: Random House.

Myers, Bernice. (1985). *Sydney Rella and the Glass Sneaker.* New York: Macmillan.

Standiford, Natalie. (1989). *The Bravest Dog Ever: The True Story of Balto.* Illustrated by Donald Cook. New York: Random House.

Sutcliffe, Jane. (2000). *Babe Didrikson Zaharias: All-Around Athlete.* Minneapolis: Carolrhoda Books.

Yolen, Jane. (1981). *Sleeping Ugly.* New York: Coward-McCann.

Chapter Books

Ada, Alma Flor. (1993). *My Name Is María Isabel.* Illustrated by K. Dyble Thompson. Translated by Ana M. Cerro. New York: Atheneum. [Early chapter book.]

Avi. (2001). *The Secret School.* San Diego: Harcourt. [Chapter book.]

Brittain, Bill. (1983). *The Wish Giver: Three Tales of Coven Tree.* Illustrated by Andrew Glass. New York: Harper & Row.

Collier, James, & Collier, Christopher. (1974). *My Brother Sam Is Dead.* New York: Four Winds.

Crisp, Marty. (2000). *My Dog, Cat.* Illustrated by True Kelley. New York: Holiday House.

Dodge, Mary Mapes. (1865). *Hans Brinker, or the Silver Skates: A Story of Life in Holland.* New York: Scribner's.

Duffey, Betsy. (1991). *A Boy in the Doghouse.* Illustrated by Leslie H. Morrill. New York: Simon & Schuster.

Duffey, Betsy. (1992). *Lucky in Left Field.* Illustrated by Leslie H. Morrill. New York: Simon & Schuster.

Forbes, Esther. (1943). *Johnny Tremain: A Novel for Young & Old.* Illustrated by Lynd Ward. Boston: Houghton Mifflin.

Fowler, Susi Gregg. (2000). *Albertina, the Animals, and Me.* Illustrated by Jim Fowler. New York: Greenwillow. [Early chapter book.]

Fox, Paula. (1991). *Monkey Island.* New York: Orchard Books.

Gardiner, John Reynolds. (1980). *Stone Fox.* Illustrated by Marcia Sewall. New York: Crowell.

Gordon, Sheila. (1987). *Waiting for the Rain.* New York: Orchard.

Hutchins, H. J. (1988). *The Three and Many Wishes of Jason Reid.* Illustrated by Julie Tennent. New York: Viking.

Koller, Jackie French. (1990). *The Dragonling.* Illustrated by Judith Mitchell. Boston: Little, Brown.

Kurtz, Jane. (1998). *The Storyteller's Beads*. San Diego: Harcourt Brace.

Levitin, Sonia. (1987). *The Return*. New York: Atheneum.

MacLachlan, Patricia. (1991). *Journey*. New York: Delacorte.

Matas, Carol. (1998). *Greater than Angels*. New York: Simon & Schuster.

Mohr, Nicholasa. (1995). *The Magic Shell*. Illustrated by Rudy Gutierrez. New York: Scholastic.

Naidoo, Beverley. (1986). *Journey to Jo'burg: A South African Story*. New York: Lippincott.

Naylor, Phyllis Reynolds. (1991). *Shiloh*. New York: Atheneum.

O'Connor, Jane. (1996). *The Bad-Luck Penny*. Illustrated by Horatio Elena. New York: Grosset & Dunlap. [Early chapter book.]

Orr, Wendy. (2000). *Ark in the Park*. Illustrated by Kerry Millard. New York: Henry Holt.

Paterson, Katherine. (1977). *Bridge to Terabithia*. Illustrated by Donna Diamond. New York: Crowell.

Pfeffer, Susan Beth. (1996). *The Trouble with Wishes*. Illustrated by Jennifer Plecas. New York: Henry Holt.

Pinkney, Andrea Davis. (1997). *Solo Girl*. Illustrated by Nneka Bennett. New York: Hyperion Books. [Early chapter book.]

Pullman, Philip. (2000). *I Was a Rat!* Illustrated by Kevin Hawkes. New York: Knopf.

Sachar, Louis. (1998). *Holes*. New York: Farrar, Straus, and Giroux.

Sachar, Louis. (2000). *A Magic Crystal?* Marvin Redpost series. New York: Random House. [Early chapter book.]

Spinelli, Jerry. (1990). *Maniac Magee*. New York: HarperTrophy.

Staples, Suzanne Fisher. (1989). *Shabanu: Daughter of the Wind*. New York: Knopf.

Temple, Frances. (1992). *Taste of Salt: A Story of Modern Haiti*. New York: Orchard.

Thomas, Jane Resh. (1987). *Fox in a Trap*. Illustrated by Troy Howell. New York: Clarion Books.

Tolan, Stephanie S. (1992). *Sophie and the Sidewalk Man*. Illustrated by Susan Avishai. New York: Four Winds Press.

Whelan, Gloria. (1988). *Silver*. Illustrated by Stephen Marchesi. New York: Random House.

Williams, Laura E. (1996). *Behind the Bedroom Wall*. Illustrated by Nancy A. Goldstein. Minneapolis: Milkweed.

Wojciechowski, Susan. (1997). *Beany (Not Beanhead) and the Magic Crystal*. Illustrated by Susanna Natti. Cambridge, MA: Candlewick Press.

Poetry

Adoff, Arnold. (1989). *Chocolate Dreams: Poems.* Illustrated by Turi MacCombie. New York: Lothrop, Lee & Shepard.

Farjeon, Eleanor. (1992). "There Isn't Time." In *Inner Chimes: Poems on Poetry* (p. 3), selected by Bobbye S. Goldstein and illustrated by Jane Breskin Zalben. Honesdale, PA: Boyds Mills Press.

Florian, Douglas. (1994). "Delicious Wishes." In Douglas Florian, *Bing Bang Boing: Poems and Drawings* (p. 52). San Diego: Harcourt Brace.

Florian, Douglas. (1994). "Fish Wish." In Douglas Florian, *Bing Bang Boing: Poems and Drawings* (p. 69). San Diego: Harcourt Brace.

Glaser, Isabel Joshlin, selector. (1995). *Dreams of Glory: Poems Starring Girls.* Illustrated by Pat Lowery Collins. New York: Atheneum.

Hoberman, Mary Ann. (1998). "Wishes." In Mary Ann Hoberman, *The Llama Who Had No Pajama: 100 Favorite Poems* (p. 12), illustrated by Betty Fraser. San Diego: Harcourt Brace.

Hughes, Langston. (1988). "Dream Variation." In *Tomie dePaola's Book of Poems* (p. 87). New York: Putnam.

Kennedy, X. J. (1988). "The Forgetful Wishing Well." In *Tomie dePaola's Book of Poems* (p. 56). New York: Putnam.

Moore, Lilian. (1992). "Poets Go Wishing." In *Inner Chimes: Poems on Poetry* (p. 6), selected by Bobbye S. Goldstein and illustrated by Jane Breskin Zalben. Honesdale, PA: Boyds Mills Press.

Informational Books

Ayer, Eleanor H., with Waterford, Helen, and Heck, Alfons. (1995). *Parallel Journeys.* New York: Atheneum.

Brenner, Barbara. (1999). *The Boy Who Loved to Draw: Benjamin West.* Illustrated by Olivier Dunrea. Boston: Houghton Mifflin.

Bridges, Ruby. (1999). *Through My Eyes.* Illustrated by Margo Lundell. New York: Scholastic.

Calmenson, Stephanie. (1994). *Rosie: A Visiting Dog's Story.* Illustrated by Justin Sutcliffe. New York: Houghton Mifflin.

Coles, Robert. (1995). *The Story of Ruby Bridges.* Illustrated by George Ford. New York: Scholastic.

Cretzmeyer, Stacy. (1994). *Your Name Is Renée: Ruth's Story as a Hidden Child: The Wartime Experiences of Ruth Kapp Hartz.* Brunswick, ME: Biddle.

Demi, author and illustrator. (1999). *Kites: Magic Wishes That Fly Up to the Sky.* New York: Crown.

Drucker, Malka, and Halperin, Michael. (1993). *Jacob's Rescue: A Holocaust Story.* New York: Bantam.

Filipovic, Zlata. (1994). *Zlata's Diary: A Child's Life in Sarajevo*. New York: Viking.

Kimmel, Elizabeth Cody. (1999). *Balto and the Great Race*. Illustrated by Nora Koerber. New York: Random House. [Nonfiction.]

Knudson, R. Rozanne. (1985). *Babe Didrikson, Athlete of the Century*. Illustrated by Ted Lewin. New York: Viking Kestrel.

Kramer, S. A. (1993). *Adventure in Alaska: An Amazing True Story of the World's Longest, Toughest Dog Sled Race*. Illustrated by Karen Meyer. New York: Bullseye.

Krull, Kathleen. (1996). *Wilma Unlimited: How Wilma Rudolph Became the World's Fastest Woman*. Illustrated by David Diaz. San Diego: Harcourt Brace.

Lobel, Anita. (1998). *No Pretty Pictures: A Child of War*. New York: Greenwillow.

Marzollo, Jean. (1993). *Happy Birthday, Martin Luther King*. Illustrated by J. Brian Pinkney. New York: Scholastic.

Miller, William. (1994). *Zora Hurston and the Chinaberry Tree*. Illustrated by Cornelius Van Wright and Ying-Hwa Hu. New York: Lee & Low Books.

Mochizuki, Ken. (1997). *Passage to Freedom: The Sugihara Story*. Illustrated by Dom Lee. New York: Lee & Low.

Perl, Lila, and Lazan, Marion Blumenthal. (1996). *Four Perfect Pebbles: A Holocaust Story*. New York: Greenwillow.

Rosenthal, Bert. (1986). *Lynette Woodard: The First Female Globetrotter*. Chicago: Children's Press.

Standiford, Natalie. (1989). *The Bravest Dog Ever: The True Story of Balto*. Illustrated by Donald Cook. New York: Random House. [Beginning reader.]

Wakeman, Nancy. (2000). *Babe Didrikson Zaharias: Driven to Win*. Minneapolis, MN: Lerner Publications.

Wood, Ted. (1996). *Iditarod Dream: Dusty and His Sled Dogs Compete in Alaska's Jr. Iditarod*. New York: Walker.

Woods, Geraldine. (1987). *Jim Henson: From Puppets to Muppets*. Minneapolis: Dillon Press.

Notes

Chapter 1

1. The legend of the Dutch boy and the dike was first told by Mary Mapes Dodge in *Hans Brinker, or the Silver Skates* published in 1865.

2. As a teacher of young children for thirty years, I have had the opportunity to explore literature with elementary-grade children and to record their contributions to the literary discussions featured in this book. The excerpts included throughout this book were drawn from the diverse discussions that have been an integral part of the read-aloud sessions in my literature program over the years.

Chapter 2

1. Witte (1992) uses the term *memorial texts* to refer to the reader's *databank* as it becomes a "multidimensional, heterarchical network of textual resources." Witte uses the term *material texts* to refer to the reader's current experiences with the text.

Chapter 7

1. For more detailed descriptions of thematic literature units, see *Teaching Literature in the Elementary School: A Thematic Approach* (Moss, 1996) and *Teaching Literature in the Middle Grades: A Thematic Approach* (Moss, 2000).

2. The story of Shiro is a Japanese tale that has been retold and included in a number of collections. The third graders featured in Chapter 7 had been introduced to "The Old Man Who Made Dead Trees Bloom" in *The Shining Princess and Other Japanese Legends* (Quayle, 1989). The children had heard this story in the context of a study of Japanese tales six months prior to the Wishes and Dreams unit.

3. Joan Aiken's *Tale of a One-Way Street and Other Stories* (1978), which includes "Bridget's Hat," was illustrated by Jan Pienkowski, who created intricate silhouettes for each of the stories in this collection.

Works Cited

Allington, R. L. (1994). The schools we have. The schools we need. *The Reading Teacher, 48*(1), 14–29.

Almasi, Janice. (1996). A new view of discussion. In L. Gambrell and J. Almasi (Eds.), *Lively discussions! Fostering engaged reading* (pp. 2–24). Newark, DE: International Reading Association.

Anderson, R., Wilson, P., and Fielding, L. (1988). Growth in reading and how children spend their time outside of school. *Reading Research Quarterly, 23*, 285–303.

Applebee, Arthur. (1989). *The teaching of literature in programs with reputations for excellence in English* (Report Series 1.1). Albany, NY: Center for the Learning and Teaching of Literature, SUNY at Albany.

Atwell, Nancie. (1987). *In the middle: Writing, reading, and learning with adolescents.* Portsmouth, NH: Heinemann.

Barrentine, S. J. (1996). Storytime plus dialogue equals interactive read alouds. In L. Gambrell and J. Almasi (Eds.), *Lively discussions! Fostering engaged reading* (pp. 52–62). Newark, DE: International Reading Association.

Baumann, J. F., Jones, L. A., & Seifert-Kessell, N. (1993). Using think alouds to enhance children's comprehension monitoring abilities. *The Reading Teacher, 47*(3), 184–193.

Beach, R. (1990). New directions in research on response to literature. In E. Farrell and J. Squire (Eds.), *Transactions with literature: A fifty-year perspective* (pp. 65–77). Urbana, IL: National Council of Teachers of English.

Bishop, R. S. (1997). Foreword. In T. Rogers and A. Soter (Eds.), *Reading across cultures: Teaching literature in a diverse society.* New York: Teachers' College Press, and Urbana, IL: National Council of Teachers of English.

Cairney, T. (1996). Pathways to meaning making: Fostering intertextuality in the classroom. In L. Gambrell and J. Almasi (Eds.). *Lively discussions! Fostering engaged reading* (pp. 170–180). Newark, DE: International Reading Association.

Campbell, J. (1949/1968). *The hero with a thousand faces.* Princeton, NJ: Princeton University Press.

Chinn, C., Anderson, R., & Waggoner, M. (2001). Patterns of discourse in two kinds of literature discussion. *Reading Research Quarterly, 36*(4), 378–411.

Chomsky, C. (1972). Stages in language development and reading exposure. *Harvard Educational Review, 42*(1), 1–33.

Clark, M. (1976). *Young fluent readers*. London: Heinemann.

Cullinan, B. (1987). *Children's literature in the reading program*. Newark, DE: International Reading Association.

Davey, B. (1983). Think aloud: Modeling the cognitive processes of reading comprehension. *Journal of Reading, 27*(1), 44–47.

Durkin, D. (1961). Children who read before grade one. *The Reading Teacher, 14*, 163–166.

Eeds, M., & Peterson, R. (1995). What teachers need to know about the literary craft. In N. Roser and M. Martinez (Eds.), *Book talk and beyond: Children and teachers respond to literature* (pp. 10–23). Newark, DE: International Reading Association.

Eeds, M., & Peterson, R. (1997). Literature studies revisited: Some thoughts on talking with children about books. *The New Advocate, 10*(1), 49–59.

Farrell, E., & Squire, J. (1990). *Transactions with literature: A fifty-year perspective*. Urbana, IL: National Council of Teachers of English.

Fink, R. (1995–96). Successful dyslexics: A constructivist study of passionate interest reading. *Journal of Adolescent and Adult Literacy, 39*(4), 268–280.

Fish, S. (1980). *Is there a text in this class? The authority of interpretive communities*. Cambridge, MA: Harvard University Press.

Gambrell, L., & Almasi, J. (Eds.). (1996). *Lively discussions! Fostering engaged reading*. Newark, DE: International Reading Association.

Hansen, J. (1987). *When writers read*. Portsmouth, NH: Heinemann.

Harste, J. (2000). Supporting critical conversations in classrooms. In K. M. Pierce (Ed.), *Adventuring with books: A booklist for pre-K–grade 6* (pp. 507–554). Urbana, IL: National Council of Teachers of English.

Hartman, D. (1995). Eight readers reading: The intertextual links of proficient readers reading multiple passages. *Reading Research Quarterly, 30*(3), 520–561.

Hepler, S., & Hickman, J. (1982). "The book was okay. I love you"—Social aspects of response to literature. *Theory into Practice, 21*(4), 278–83.

Hickman, J., & Cullinan, B. (Eds.). (1989). *Children's literature in the classroom: Weaving Charlotte's web*. Needham Heights, MA: Christopher-Gordon.

Higonnet, M. R. (1990). The playground of the peritext. *Children's Literature Association Quarterly, 15*(2), 47–49.

Holdaway, Don. (1979). *The foundations of literacy*. Sydney, Australia: Ashton Scholastic.

Huck, C. (1982). "I give you the end of a golden string." *Theory into Practice, 21*(4), 315–321.

Hunt, L. C. (1970/1996–1997). The effect of self-esteem, interest, and motivation upon independent, instructional, and frustrational levels. *The Reading Teacher, 50*(4), 278–282.

Langer, J. (1990). Understanding literature. *Language Arts, 67*(8), 812–16.

Langer, J. (1994). A response-based approach to reading literature. *Language Arts, 71*(3), 203–211.

Langer, J. (1995). *Envisioning literature: Literary understanding and literature instruction.* New York: Teachers' College Press.

Langford, J. C., & Allen, E. G. (1983). The effects of USSR on students' attitudes and achievement. *Reading Horizons, 23*(3), 194–200.

Leland, C., & Harste, J. (2000). Critical literacy: Enlarging the space of the possible. *Primary Voices K–6, 9*(2) 3–7.

Lukens, R. J. (1999). *A critical handbook of children's literature* (6th ed.). New York: Longman.

McGee, L. M. (1995). Talking about books with young children. In N. Roser and M. Martinez (Eds.), *Book talk and beyond: Children and teachers respond to literature* (pp. 105–115). Newark, DE: International Reading Association.

McGee, L. M. (1996). Response-centered talk: Windows on children's thinking. In L. Gambrell and J. Almasi (Eds.), *Lively discussions! Fostering engaged reading* (pp. 194–207). Newark, DE: International Reading Association.

McKenna, M., Ellsworth, R. A., & Kear, D. (1995). Children's attitudes toward reading: A national survey. *Reading Research Quarterly, 30*(4), 934–957.

Moreillon, J. (1999). The candle and the mirror: One author's journey as an outsider. *The New Advocate, 12*(2), 127–140.

Moss, J. F. (1995). Preparing focus units with literature: Crafty foxes and authors' craft. In N. Roser and M. Martinez (Eds.), *Book talk and beyond: Children and teachers respond to literature* (pp. 53–65). Newark, DE: International Reading Association.

Moss, J. F. (1996). *Teaching literature in the elementary school: A thematic approach.* Norwood, MA: Christopher-Gordon.

Moss, J. F. (2000). *Teaching literature in the middle grades: A thematic approach* (2nd ed.). Norwood, MA: Christopher-Gordon.

Oster, L. (2001). Using the think aloud for reading instruction. *The Reading Teacher, 55*(1), 64–69.

Paley, V. (1981). *Wally's stories: Conversations in the kindergarten.* Cambridge, MA: Harvard University Press.

Probst, Robert E. (1990). *Literature as Exploration* and the classroom. In E. J. Farrell and J. R. Squire (Eds.), *Transactions with literature: A fifty-year perspective* (pp. 27–37). Urbana, IL: National Council of Teachers of English.

Rosenblatt, L. (1938/1976). *Literature as exploration* (3rd ed.). New York: Noble and Noble.

Rosenblatt, L. (1978). *The reader, the text, and the poem.* Carbondale: Southern Illinois University Press.

Rosenblatt, L. (1982). The literary transaction: Evocation and response. *Theory into Practice, 21*(4) 268–277. Reprinted in K. E. Holland, R. A. Hungerford, & S. B. Ernst (Eds.), *Journeying: Children responding to literature* (pp. 6–23), Portsmouth, NH: Heinemann.

Roser, N. L., & Martinez, M. G. (Eds.). (1995). *Book talk and beyond: Children and teachers respond to literature.* Newark, DE: International Reading Association.

Sipe, L. (2000). "Those two gingerbread boys could be brothers": How children use intertextual connections during storybook readalouds. *Children's Literature in Education, 31*(2), 73–90.

Sipe, L. (2002). Talking back and taking over: Young children's expressive engagement during storybook read-alouds. *The Reading Teacher, 55*(5), 476–483.

Smith, F. (1978). *Understanding reading: A psycholinguistic analysis of reading and learning to read* (2nd ed.). New York: Holt, Rinehart and Winston.

Smith, F. (1984). Reading like a writer. In J. M. Jensen (Ed.), *Composing and comprehending.* Urbana, IL: ERIC Clearinghouse on Reading and Communication Skills and the National Conference on Research in English.

Smith, F. (1988). *Understanding reading: A psycholinguistic analysis of reading and learning to read* (4th ed.). Hillsdale, NJ: Lawrence Erlbaum Associates.

Thorndike, R. (1973). *Reading comprehension, education in 15 countries: An empirical study.* International Studies in Evaluation (Vol. 3). New York: Wiley.

Tiedt, I. M. (2000). *Teaching with picture books in the middle school.* Newark, DE: International Reading Association.

Turner, J. C. (1995). The influence of classroom contexts on young children's motivation for literacy. *Reading Research Quarterly, 30*(3), 410–441.

Vygotsky, L. S. (1962/1986). *Thought and language.* Cambridge, MA: MIT Press.

Vygotsky, L. S. (1978). *Mind in society: Development of higher psychological processes.* Cambridge, MA: Winthrop.

Wade, S. (1990). Using think alouds to assess comprehension. *The Reading Teacher, 44*(7), 442–451.

Wells, D. (1995). Leading grand conversations. In N. Roser and M. Martinez (Eds.), *Book talk and beyond: Children and teachers respond to literature* (pp. 132–139). Newark, DE: International Reading Association.

Wells, G. (1986). *The meaning makers: Children learning language and using language to learn.* Portsmouth, NH: Heinemann.

Wigfield, A., & Guthrie, J. T. (1995). *Dimensions of children's motivations for reading: An initial study* (Research Rep. No. 34). Athens, GA: Universities of Georgia and Maryland, National Reading Research Center.

Witte, S. P. (1992). "Context, text, intertext: Toward a constructivist semiotic of writing." *Written Communication*, 9(2), 237–308.

Wolf, D. (1988). *Reading reconsidered: Literature and literacy in high school.* New York: College Entrance Examination Board.

Yolen, J. (2000). *Touch magic: Fantasy, faerie and folklore in the literature of childhood.* Little Rock, AR: August House.

Index

Author

After several years as a classroom teacher and then as a reading teacher, **Joy F. Moss** became the literature specialist for the elementary division of a private school in Rochester, New York. As a cross-grade teacher, she introduced a literature program into the school curriculum twenty years ago and has been exploring literature with children ever since.

Moss has also been actively involved as a teacher educator. Since 1970, she has taught graduate students as well as undergraduates at the Warner Graduate School of Education and Human Development, University of Rochester, where she has an appointment as adjunct associate professor. During this time she has conducted a variety of inservice courses for schools in and around Rochester. As a teacher educator, Moss has focused on the translation of theories of literary and literacy learning into classroom practice.

Moss has drawn on her work with young learners and students of learning to write articles for professional journals, chapters for edited texts, and several books.

Moss and her husband have three children and nine grandchildren. They all love books.

This book was typeset in Palatino and Helvetica by Electronic Imaging.
The typefaces used on the cover were Adobe Garamond, Adobe Myriad,
and Emigre Ottomat.
The book was printed on 50-lb. Williamsburg Offset by Versa Press, Inc.